Dr. Klaus Volkamer · Weighing Soul Substance

Dr. Klaus Volkamer

WEIGHING SOUL SUBSTANCE

BROSOWSKI
PUBLISHING

Bibliographic information published by the Deutsche Nationalbibliothek
The Deutsche Nationalbibliothek lists this publication in the Deutsche Nationalbibliografie; detailed bibliographic data are available on the Internet at http://dnb.dnb.de.

ISBN 978-3-946533-02-3

©2020 by BROSOWSKI Publishing, Berlin Germany
www.brosowski-publishing.com
e-mail: info@brosowski-publishing.com

Edited by Dr. Kenneth Walton, Fairfield IA, USA
Layout and cover design Sascha Krenzin, Berlin Germany

Contents

Preface

It is commonly known that the Greek philosopher Democritus stated about 2500 years ago that all visible matter is composed of atomic particles which cannot be further divided. Not widely known is the fact that Democritus also postulated the existence of an invisible subtle matter built up of indivisible atoms, and that this invisible matter constitutes the human soul. While Democritus' atomic hypothesis of ordinary matter is today a fundamental understanding in physics, his second prediction, of an invisible additional form of matter, is unknown to modern science.

Another statement about an invisible substance comes from the ancient Vedic tradition of knowledge as related by Vedic Master and scholar Maharishi Mahesh Yogi. Maharishi describes the existence of an invisible, semi-liquid form of matter called "Soma". He mentions two aspects of Soma: first as the carrier of consciousness and second as the building material of the universe. This view suggests the possibility of a scientific bridge between consciousness and physics.

These statements from classical Greece and ancient India inspired the research program to experimentally verify invisible matter that is reported in this book. The experimental approach used to achieve this was state-of-the-art, high-precision, automatic weighing technology accompanied by the use of special detectors that absorb or emit this invisible form of matter we named "subtle matter". This method not only allowed the objective proof of existence of subtle matter, but also allowed its characterization. Indivisible quanta of this form of matter were demonstrated, and so were associations of such quanta. It turned out that subtle matter exhibits a field-like structure with macroscopic, i.e. weighable, mass. This matter exists in two forms: a form that increases the weight of the detector and was assigned a positive sign, and a form that decreases the weight of the detector and was assigned a negative sign. Subtle matter is omnipresent in our local or global environment and beyond. Our experiments led us to posit that any entity, from atoms to the known life forms, celestial bodies or even invisible angels, possesses a "body" of subtle matter that may represent the "soul". It also appears that the invisible mass of subtle matter can be used as a new and omnipresent source of free energy having no negative side effects on the environment or climate.

Dozens of our fascinating experimental results with subtle matter await you in this story of discovery. These results have led to coherent scientific explanations of paranormal and other states of human consciousness, of near death or out of body experiences, and exact mathematical predictions of the values of natural constants. In addition, the two forms of subtle matter are objectively verified candidates for the Dark Matter and Dark Energy proposed by cosmologists. This detection and proposed understanding of subtle matter represent a breakthrough of present-day science into previously unreachable realms of natural law and of human and universal life.

I would like to thank the following individuals for their invaluable help as described: Dr. Kenneth Walton, Fairfield, Iowa, USA, without whom this book was not possible, for copy-editing and constantly rewriting the text to ensure a good read; my publisher, Horst Brosowski, Berlin, Germany, for excellent cooperation throughout; Sascha Krenzin for the layout and cover design; Alexander Fisken for not getting tired from proof reading, Sylvio Crone, Paul Schläpfer and many others for contributing ideas and inspiring concepts to the content of this book.

Dr. Klaus Volkamer 2020, Frankenthal, Germany

1 Is the Soul Made of Subtle Matter?

In this book, you will read about a material that cannot be seen, touched, smelled, heard, or tasted, but surprisingly can be weighed! We are attempting to give scientific proof of a reality that is beyond the senses. The book provides an elaborate extension of today's view of the world based on scientific experiments that reveal a reality far greater than the one presented in modern physics.

We are talking about the discovery of a previously unknown form of matter, one that is new to our modern scientific world but, paradoxically, has been known to some for a very long time.

History has recorded the existence of subtle realms of life, but our school textbooks have either intentionally omitted them or forgotten to mention them. Plato, for example, spoke about a "primordial form of matter". Aristotle reported on the existence of a kind of matter that he termed *"materia prima"*. Democritus described, besides the visible matter of common objects, a kind of invisible matter that he considered to be the origin of consciousness and emotions.

A type of subtle or invisible matter is also present in other ancient traditions of knowledge. Thus, masters of those traditions in our times, such as Maharishi Mahesh Yogi from the ancient Vedic tradition, or the present Dalai Lama from the ancient Tibetan tradition, have reported on such forms of matter. Maharishi Mahesh Yogi has described a kind of invisible, "semi-liquid" substance termed "Soma" which is discussed in the Vedic literature. This Soma is deeply connected with consciousness in its purest state, itself regarded as the very source of all that exists.

Also other historic researchers and scientists have reported on categories of reality that are invisible, yet exhibit quite unusual properties basic to human life. For example, both Giordano Bruno and Wilhelm Leibniz described indivisible "monades". Nikola Tesla, Viktor Schauberger, Rudolf Steiner, Charles W. Leadbeater, Erwin László, Maria Thun, Emoto, Hauschka, David Bohm, Rupert Sheldrake, and others have discussed evidence that more exists than the eye can see.

This "invisible kind of matter" has been given various names because each researcher may be dealing with different aspects or may have called it by a different name based on the language of their time and tradition. Some of these names that you might have heard are Veda, Apeiron, Psi, Tao, Logos, Ether, *vis vitalis*, *materia prima*, radiations, soma, to name just a few.

These statements, and especially those from the ancient Vedic tradition of India, inspired our high-precision weighing experiments that finally led, after about 35 years of research, to the proof of a previously unknown kind of matter, which we have named "subtle matter", that is presented in this book.

However, the question as to whether or not this subtle matter discovered through weighing experiments is equivalent to that described by all the above-mentioned ancient seers and researchers is beyond the scope of this book to answer. In fact, that topic could constitute a completely new book. Nevertheless, it should be noted that at this stage our research has already identified different forms of subtle matter – and further forms are expected as research continues.

Our high-precision weighing tests have discovered that subtle matter exhibits properties that are different from the properties of normal matter, and are not identical with the properties of any of the sub-microscopic particles known to modern physics. The detected quanta of this subtle form of matter have a field-like quality, which extends spatially (for details see chapter 4, Summary and Appendix).

In our experiments, subtle matter exhibits two kinds of macroscopic mass effects: one that increases weight, which will be called in this book "positive subtle matter" and one that decreases weight, called "negative subtle matter". Surprisingly, we found that the weight decreasing ("negative") form of subtle matter clearly has a health promoting or life supporting influence on living systems.

On the other hand, the weight-increasing, positive form exhibits the opposite qualities. Tests on biological systems have led us to characterize subtle matter with a positive sign as "entropic" and health damaging in its effects. And subtle matter with a negative sign as health promoting or "negentropic" in its effects, indicating it is reducing entropy.

This book will take you through some of the experiments leading to the surprising discovery of these special qualities of subtle matter.

Chapter 2 will show results from tests with living systems. Besides tests with regular persons, you will see results from healers and advanced meditation practitioners. In the same first section you will also find surprising results from a new alternative healing technique, called Aura Surgery. These measurements led to the discovery that, in addition to its body of gross matter, every living being is carrying also a body made of subtle matter. This subtle body may represent the life-force, the aura, or the soul. It acts as a kind of pilot-field that operates the gross body like a pilot controls an airplane.

Furthermore, you will see that such a pilot-field also was found in plants and can be expected for animals as well. This section also gives a bit of evidence for "celestial life". For example, you will find a dramatic weight reduction (due to negentropic subtle matter) of a person with paranormal abilities during the time when she claims to have been "touched" by a celestial being.

Chapter 3 will provide evidence that not only do living beings carry an invisible subtle field but also so do objects in nature that are said to be "inanimate". This subtle matter was not only detected in purely physical or chemical systems, but it soon became clear that the Earth itself and also the Sun, Moon, and all other celestial objects are carrying subtle field-bodies which are influencing each other on a constant basis.

In **Chapter 4**, the interested reader will find a short summary and also detailed information about the experimental equipment and procedures of our research, as well as articles with summaries of other basic topics like "Phase Boundaries", "Properties of Subtle Matter", etc. The book ends with the **Appendix** presenting some special scientific papers dealing with the physical and mathematical basis and interpretation of our results. It is simply not possible to present all the results from over 35 years of research in one book. In this volume you will find, in an easy to understand style, an introduction to the basic discoveries about subtle matter. The depth of information is hopefully adjusted so that a nonscientist reader will be able to understand.

In case this overview to our research raises the desire to go deeper into details of the experiments and also into the quantum mechanical analysis of subtle matter, we recommend having a look at the Appendix.

Furthermore, the scientific reader might like to consult our books:

▷ *Discovery of Subtle Matter – A Short Introduction*
Klaus Volkamer 2017; ISBN 978-3-946533-01-6

▷ or our upcoming book on *science and subtle matter* whose publication is planned for 2021.

2 Discovering the Role of Subtle Matter in Life

Every living being be it human, animal, or plant, possesses, besides its visible gross body a superimposed invisible subtle body. Throughout time many traditions have believed in the existence of an invisible Aura and Soul, or Spirit of every individual. For reasons of clarity, we will call the subtle body a "field-body" or "pilot-field" from now on.

This invisible field-body permeates the visible, gross body or may be superimposed on it. For the first time in human history our research has shown that the field-bodies have real, measurable mass, as well as energy and information content. In the following we will study the effects of such field-bodies, as they are measured in precision weighing experiments.

2.1 Does the Soul Leave the Body During Sleep?

Again and again people report having temporarily left their body – i.e. during the so called Near Death Experiences (NDE) or Out of Body Experiences (OBE). Throughout history also reports can be found of people who claim that they, or their soul, are able to travel at will to other realms of reality during sleep, meditation or trance.

Our research proves that subtle matter can attach and detach itself from gross matter, and one would expect it to do so with the human body in the same manner as it appears to do with gross matter, with plants and with planets. Therefore it might be interesting to look at some weighing experiments with people during sleep.

Fig. 1: Weighing a sleeping subject

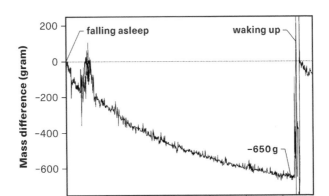

In such an experiment, as recorded in Fig. 1, the test subject was resting quietly face up while being weighed, together with the bed, once every second using a balance (termed "bed-balance"; see Section 4.2, Weighing Equipment). This bed-balance consisted of four high precision balances, one under each foot of the bed, which were electronically connected via special computer software. Thereby the weight could be recorded with an accuracy of plus or minus 0.2 gram.

A continuous weight decrease was detected starting from the moment sleep began and reached about − 650 g over the 13-minute sleep period. Upon waking, a positive dramatic weight-jump of about +650 g occurred, taking the weight approximately back to the original baseline. Modern physics cannot explain such large mass changes. It should be clear that this result on the bed-balance is not explicable as merely body movements during sleep. No movement during sleep is imaginable such that a person loses 650 grams of weight over a period of 13 minutes and then gains it back within a few seconds while waking up.

Weight variations of about plus or minus 20 grams are due to breathing and body movements during sleep. In the process of awakening, after about 13 minutes in this case, involuntary body movements lead to strong oscillations or fluctuations of weight, as can be seen at the end of the graph. Also the data cannot be explained by loss of water due to breathing or transpiration (as will be seen more clearly in Fig. 2).

These results suggest that the human body consists not only of gross matter, but also of a form of subtle matter that can be emitted and reabsorbed fully or in parts over short time intervals. From our point of view, the possibility should be considered that a subtle field-body with positive weight, or part of such a body, left the gross body for awhile. Another theoretical possibility might be some sort of levitation effect.

Fig. 2 shows the test-results of another experiment with a person sleeping quietly on the bed-balance. This test showed a typical slow decline in mean weight of about 20 grams per 20 minutes during sleep, likely explained by the loss of water through breathing and transpiration.

Fig. 2: Another experiment with a sleeping subject

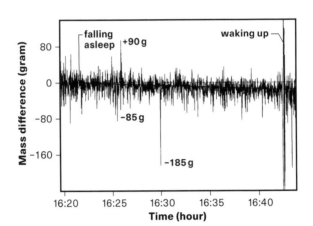

The rapid variations of weight of about plus or minus 20 grams, are again due to the activity of breathing and other small body movements during sleep. In the process of awakening after about 25 minutes, seen at the end of the graph, again involuntary body movements lead to strong bidirectional fluctuations of weight. But our knowledge from traditional physics cannot explain the larger unidirectional mass changes with observed peak deviations of −85 grams, +90 grams and −185 grams.

From the measured data, it looks to us that an unknown mass with a weight of 85 grams and a few minutes later even a mass of 185 gram was able to leave the body in an instant for a short period and then return. The question must arise: what could this be? Could it be a part of the soul or aura disconnecting from the body and traveling somewhere?

Another question is what might have happened in the moment when the weight jumped up by about 90 grams? Could this be a hint that something visited the sleeping person? From close analysis of the data, it is not possible that these jumps occur due to sudden body movements. Such movements of the body would show as similar plus and minus fluctuations to those seen at the end during the waking up phase of the test.

Fig. 3: More sleep research

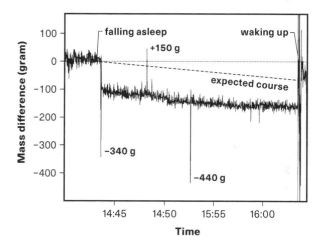

Fig. 3 shows another interesting effect that was found in a weighing experiment with a person sleeping on the bed-balance. In this graph we have added as a dashed line the course of the weighing data that could be expected from the smooth decline of weight due to loss of water from breathing and transpiration.

However, a few minutes after falling asleep, a rapid weight-jump occurred with a weight drop of about 340 gram. This was followed by a positive weight-jump upwards, but not back to the starting level. The subject's weight then remained on a level near −150 gram for more than one hour and from that time on almost followed a parallel course to the expected dashed line, but at lower weights. In addition, strong peaks with significant further stepwise deviations occurred during the experiment. At the moment the subject woke up, again the weight immediately jumped back upwards to the normal, expected range.

These observed deviations can be explained if one proposes that the gross body of the tested person also carries an invisible field-body of a previously unknown subtle matter with measurable mass.

The question may arise, at this point, why different persons show different intensities of weight changes? This opens up a vast future field of detailed and extended sleep-research. From our experiments to date, it only can be said that a previously unknown mass influence of subtle matter has been discovered and clearly violates the physical law of conservation of mass.

Subtle matter is, according to our research, obviously a field-like phenomenon that displays a constant interaction with surrounding subtle fields. This interplay of subtle matter fields with normal matter can produce a wide range of experimental results that are hard to explain.

The influence of mental activity or of broader environmental conditions can be expected to affect the interaction of a sleeping person with subtle matter fields. Furthermore, there is evidence from other experiments that subtle influences from the Sun, Moon, solar planets, and constellations are constantly interacting with the subtle body of people during sleep.

The subtle body appears to be, to some extent, reversibly separate from the gross sleeping body. These results might prove the saying that during sleep the "soul travels to the Universe or to Heaven". On the other hand, the question may arise as to whether the occasional upward weight jumps indicate that the field-body we propose may be the soul gets nourishment or information from cosmic subtle fields, or is even "visited" by other subtle entities.

Such weighing experiments should be expanded in special long-term research. These weight measurements of sleeping persons may open new areas of sleep research. Some questions of interest could be, for example: do the weight changes of a person asleep correlate with measurements of heart rate variability (HRV), rapid eye movements (REM), electro-dermal activity (EDA), electroencephalography measurements (EEG), or blood pressure etc.

Fig. 4 displays various subtle structures of the human field-body. The field-body has weighable mass and is superimposed on the visible gross body. From our theoretical data analysis of subtle matter, we are expecting that the field-body is rotating about the gross body with high velocity (maybe with light speed).

Fig. 4: Man's invisible, rotating field-body, i.e. the "pilot-field"

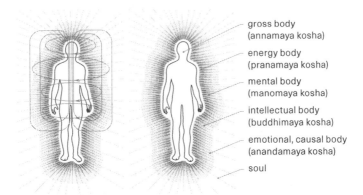

gross body
(annamaya kosha)

energy body
(pranamaya kosha)

mental body
(manomaya kosha)

intellectual body
(buddhimaya kosha)

emotional, causal body
(anandamaya kosha)

soul

This seems to hold for all subtle field-bodies bound to gross objects. The finer structures within the field-body, as shown above, have already been described from ancient Vedic seers as various subtle "shells" (i.e. "koshas") with different functions, see also the book of Charles W. Leadbeater "Man visible and invisible".

The field-body of a person can also be subjectively detected by "feeling it". To do this, two persons should stand quietly face to face at arm's length, with eyes closed and with arms hanging down. Now, person A, who wants to detect the field-body of person B, should slowly raise both arms to a horizontal position on each side of his body, holding the palms in a vertical position. Without much concentration, but with alertness, person A should start to very slowly close in both arms in the direction of person B. Usually there comes a position of the two arms of person A, where person A starts to feel a weak resistance.

At this point the interaction between the field-bodies of the hands reaches an intensity that becomes detectable for person A as weak resistance to further movement of the arms. This does not mean that now the complete spatial extension of the field-body of person B has been detected, but an indication of the existence of B's field-body may thus be realized.

2.2   Healers Radiate Subtle Matter: Scientific Evidence

In the previous section we presented a few examples and some considerations of our sleep research experiments. Now we will take a look at the first evidence that people with special mental abilities can produce, focus, and direct subtle matter.

To measure the possibility of influencing the weight of objects by mental power, we had to change the weighing technology. In these experiments we worked with specially designed "detectors" and scales which are able to register even minimal changes of weight.

Fig. 5 shows the results of such weight measurements with a high precision, two-pan laboratory scale (type Micro M25-D-V from the company Sartorius AG, Germany) with a reproducibility of 1 to 2 micrograms (1 "**microgram**" equals one millionth of a gram; in some graphs you will see "**milligram**": 1 milligram equals one thousandth of a gram or one thousand micrograms; for more information about the scales see Section 4.2, Weighing Equipment). One pan weighed the detector which was in this case a gas-tight sealed glass flask with internal silver plating.

Fig. 5: Measuring the healer's "Beam of Sight"

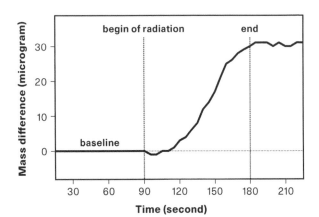

During our experiments we found that the internal silver plating of glass flasks is a very suitable method to create a so called "phase boundary" at which subtle matter binds easily (see Section 4.3, Phase Boundaries and Section 4.4, Detectors for Subtle Matter).

The production of "internal silver plating" is a standard procedure from chemistry in which a glass flask is filled with two chemicals that, when mixed together, produce a thin layer of pure silver on the inside wall of the glass container (it looks like a kind of Christmas ball). The phase boundary in this case is the contact area between the glass wall and the metallic silver coating. In general all such areas between the layers of two different substances work as "phase boundaries" at which, for as yet unknown reasons, the subtle matter tends to bind easily. A metallic reference sample of the same weight without any generated phase boundaries was placed in the other pan.

The graph in Fig. 5 shows the difference in weight (here called "mass difference") between the detector and the control sample during the time of the experiment. As can be seen above, in the beginning (before the healer started to act), the mass difference between the detector and the reference sample on the other side of the scale remained constant.

This is expected from physics: the weight of a gas tight sealed flask should not change in the course of time. The complete scale itself was even covered in a closed box and fully protected from any outside influence (see again 4.2, Weighing Equipment).

So first a perfect constant baseline between the weights of the two samples was measured. After 90 seconds a person with healing abilities started to direct his hands and the focus of his sight towards the detector from a distance of about 50 cm away from the scale. In the above graph it can be seen very clearly that, when the healer directed his hands and eye focus on the detector for about 90 seconds, the detector's weight increased rapidly up to +30 micrograms ("μg") and remained at that level even after the healer had stopped influencing the scale and left the room.

In our view this mathematically highly significant mass-change indicates that from the healer's hands and/

or his focus of view, some kind of unknown subtle matter radiation was emitted and was absorbed by the detector. Similar results were obtained in further experiments by directing only the healer's eye focus on the detector. This indicates the existence of a subtle "Beam of Sight" (already described by Plato and Epicurus) emitted from the human eyes, as well as a "Beam of Touch" emitted by the hands.

Nonscientists might ask, at this point, why a change of 30 microgram ("µg") difference is considered to be significant and what it might prove. What does a change of weight in the range of a few micrograms mean? One microgram is a really very small mass; it is just one millionth of a gram. Or in other words, one million micrograms makes up one gram. So when we talk about a 30 microgram weight change, normally nobody would notice or care about such a small difference.

However, the challenge with this and our following measurement results is that in science we have to consider one of the most fundamental laws, which is called **"the law of conservation of mass"** or **"principle of mass conservation".** It states that for any system closed to all transfers of matter and energy, the mass of the system must remain constant over time. Hence, the quantity of mass is always conserved over time under ambient conditions.

Furthermore the law implies that mass can neither be created out of nothing nor can it dissolve to nothing. It can only change for example to heat or energy (exceptions are found only in high energetic atomic reactions).

This law is so fundamental to modern science that a mysterious mass change "out of the blue" is considered by scientists to be absolutely impossible because this would violate the law of conservation of mass. It would normally be considered to be a measuring mistake that in an isolated scale at a constant temperature and pressure, the weight of the detector compared to a reference sample could change by any amount.

It was a great problem for the scientific community when recently the International Prototype Kilogram standard sample that was stored since 1889 in Paris, showed a mass reduction of about 50 micrograms (probably caused by cleaning procedures like scratches or other unknown influences). Similar mass changes also were recorded from copies of the prototype that are stored in the US and other countries. Due to these problems in 2018, a huge worldwide project took place to set up a new prototype.

Therefore it is not surprising that the majority of scientists will not even take a look at our results let alone to try and repeat the experiments – even though such mass anomalies have been reported again and again in the past 100 years.

Also, we should not forget that these small mass amounts contain a huge amount of energy. According to Einstein's famous and commonly known formula $E = m \cdot c^2$, matter, i.e. "m", can be converted under proper conditions into energy, i.e. "E".

If we assume that 30 µg of subtle matter could be completely transformed into heat we come to the following conclusions. According to Einstein's formula, if we multiply 30 µg by the speed of light squared, we get heat energy "E" of nearly 2,700,000 kJ.

It is beyond the scope of this book to go into mathematical details, but our calculations reveal that even very small amounts of subtle matter, like 30 µg, if transformed into heat, could for example easily heat a complete swimming pool or household in the winter. This suggests that the small detected weight deviation may contain a huge amount of energy. This would be a big problem for traditional science!

Fig. 6 shows the change in sample mass difference measured after the healer had ended the experiment shown above in Fig. 5. For clarity we have shown those previous results on the left of this graph. After measuring the baseline, the healer from time A to time B focused his hands and eyes on the balance and produced a significant weight increase of about 30 micrograms as already described. At the end of the experiment (point B in Fig. 6) the healer left the room and relaxed quietly sitting on a chair in an adjoining room (about 4 meters from the balance).

As he reported later, after another 65 s (at position C) he just started to focus his mental attention on the detector at the still running balance in the adjoining room with the intention that now a weight loss should occur. And it worked. The weight of the detector dropped by more than 35 micrograms, even below the values of the baseline that was recorded prior to the test, possibly due to the healer's intention that the weight should now drop. This is consistent with the existence of a subtle "Beam of Thought". These experimental results give a possible causal physical explanation for Rupert Sheldrake's arguments presented in his book "The Sense of Being Stared At", 2003.

Fig. 6: A "Beam of Thought" from outside the room

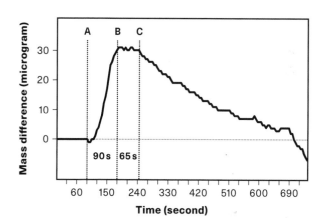

The results of Fig. 5 show that even the focus of view alone ("Beam of Sight") can produce measurable mass changes. Similar results were also obtained when a "normal person" with no special healing abilities performed such a test, as can be seen in Fig. 7. However the measured effects were smaller.

The previous weighing experiments with sleeping persons as shown in the beginning of this chapter inspired the next experiment in which we weighed a healer and found that he could change his weight just by mental processes.

27

Fig. 7: Another weighable "Beam of Sight"

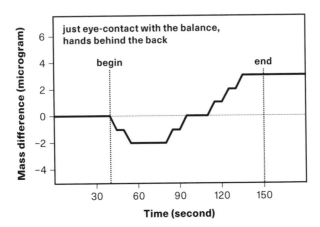

Fig. 8 depicts the change in mass difference of a person with strong healing abilities who was weighed on a sensitive chair-balance (see Section 4.2, Weighing Equipment), to an accuracy of plus or minus 0.1 g with automatic data recording.

The quietly sitting person thought intensively of various emotionally disagreeable or emotionally agreeable encounters with situations and persons. While these mental processes took place, intensive mass changes of his body, up to −900 grams were observed. First the person was sitting quietly from time period A to B. His weight was fluctuating due to breath movements within an expected range producing an accurate baseline. From period B to C the person thought about an emotionally very unpleasant, painful social situation and his weight increased constantly up to +300 grams.

Fig. 8: A Healer influencing the weight of his body

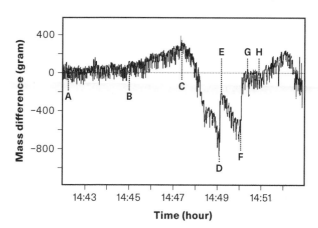

In period C to F however, the healer thought about two different beloved, yet absent persons, and the healer's weight reduced dramatically from period C to D by about 900 grams! At time D the person stopped thinking about the first beloved friend, and the weight again went up from D to E by about 300 grams.

While thinking about another beloved friend in period E to F, again a mass decrease occurred of about 200 grams. After thinking about this friend stopped, at position F, the weight of the healer again increased until nearly reaching the baseline. Finally during period F to H "heavenly beings" were mentally contacted and this was followed by an increase in weight.

Human consciousness identical with the weighable field-body? In addition to the results of our weighing experiments with sleeping persons, these dramatic results provide strong evidence for the existence of a

29

weighable subtle body field of humans and its connectedness to processes in the human psyche. The experiments in this chapter indicate that the subtle body is clearly connected with the consciousness of the individual. These results appear to support the hypothesis that human consciousness is either identical with the subtle matter field-body or is closely connected with the internal structures of this field-body. Various conditions of consciousness are reflected on the gross weighable level of the person and can interact over a distance on physical objects, i.e., for example, from a person to the detector being weighted on the scale.

In this book **the term "consciousness"** is mentioned frequently. Consequently, it is important to give some meaning to the term in the context of subtle matter. Theories of "consciousness" or "awareness" have existed since ancient times. Those theories range from "consciousness as a property of the brain" to "consciousness as the primary field underlying all that exists." This latter meaning could be better called "pure consciousness" or "pure awareness". This state is called "pure" because it is abstract, free of activity or content and yet is the source of the active consciousness of humans and other beings. This is like the role attributed to the "unified field" of modern theoretical physics. The unified field cannot be directly measured but is understood to be the source of the elementary particles that constitute all ordinary matter. In this book, "consciousness" mainly is used in its vibrating, individualized form, because this is the type that is measurable.

Modern science tries to explain human consciousness as resulting from interactions of neuronal networks and synaptic processes in the brain. Our research into subtle matter, on the other hand, reveals that consciousness may express first through internal activities of the human field-body which could, in turn, guide processes in the brain. This understanding leads to the conclusion that the brain is just a resonance instrument to the human subtle body "psyche" which is part of the field-body.

We therefore hypothesize that the invisible field-body is the guiding pilot-field of the visible gross body and represents the human psyche, directly expressing consciousness and vital force. This subtle field-body is constantly interacting with the surrounding subtle matter fields which, themselves, reflect a kind of collective consciousness involving many souls.

This seems to hold also for the totality of the gross body and all its internal microbiological processes which all seem to be permanently guided by processes of the subtle matter field-body, starting from the first fertilized egg to the end of life for human beings, animals and plants. These hypotheses will be discussed more in the following chapters.

We must emphasize that these speculations apparently supported by our first experiments should be the subject of a much more varied and detailed program of weighing research.

The previously described experiments suggest that emission of subtle-matter radiation can take place, via the eyes as subtle "beams of non-electromagnetic radiation", i.e. a kind of "fine light". One might also say, the ears emit subtle "hearing-beams", the hands or feet subtle "beams of touch", and the brain subtle "beams of thought". The hair and nails of our hands and feet are made of a special protein, termed keratin. It is formed of protein triple-helices that are wound to form stiff superhelices, the perfect spiral geometry which is an excellent "container" for subtle "fine light".

Therefore, with the hands we can, in principle, "feel" subtle matter fields around objects or around living beings. And by petting the head of a person, a field-field interaction occurs that may have calming psycho-somatic effects.

A subtle Beam of Sight. The ancient Greek philo-sophers such as Plato and Epicurus proposed in their "emission theory" that human beings and animals would need a "Beam of Sight", emitted from the eyes and reflected from a gross object, in addition to the reflected electromagnetic light from the Sun, to perceive an object.

In this view, visual perception needs both forms of radiation, that is, beams of subtle matter and beams of normal electromagnetic light from the Sun or other emit-ters. If one of the two beams is missing in the neuronal processing of visual perception, a person becomes blind. This may happen when the specific brain area for one of the two beams of radiation is damaged, perhaps due to an accident, while the neuronal processing of the other radiation is still functioning in another area of the brain.

Fig. 9: Subtle matter radiation from the human body

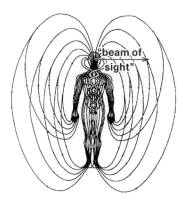

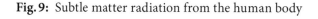

The left sketch results from
a cross section through the
revolving non-electromagnetic
subtle torus, see below,
shaping the human field-body.

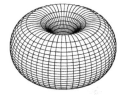

In modern psychology this condition is known as "visual agnosia". If one tries to throw a ball into the face of a person with visual agnosia, it can happen that the ball is warded off by the person spontaneously raising their hand, because the visual reflex via the brain stem still functions. But if one asks the person why he or she raised their hand, the answer may be "I don't know". The approaching ball was not consciously seen because the information from the subtle matter beam was missing.

Could microbiological structures in the photoreceptor cells of the human eye be found from where a beam of subtle matter radiation might be emitted and reabsorbed? These structures might be found by studying the microscopic anatomy of human eye's photoreceptors, i.e. the membrane shelves with light-sensors, the geometrical highly ordered structure of energy-supplying mitochondria and of protein-spirals in the light receptors and so on. Indeed, there are multiple cellular components that are built up of highly ordered geo-metrical structures. Due to their form-specific interaction, quanta of subtle matter interact especially quickly and well with such geometric structures from which they could be emitted during the visual process. Thus, it can be expected that within the detailed structure of cells of the eye, microbiological areas can be located from which a beam of subtle-matter radiation could be generated and emitted.

Similarly, in the brain, spiral structures wound around the nerve cell-extensions are expected to be excellent absorbers of subtle matter and might provide suitable locations for emitting a thought beam of subtle matter. Even though it is clear that the details of these processes must be elucidated by future research, the above mentioned microbiological structures in the eye and in the human brain support the concept that a superposition of electromagnetic and subtle matter effects could provide a critical component of visual perception in human beings and animals.

There is yet another aspect of the human visual process that deserves examination. In the usual waking state of a person, normal electromagnetic (light) radiation effects appear to dominate the visual process, even though the eye's unconscious processes of emitted and re-absorbed beams of subtle matter are essential for conscious recognition of an object. However, if a person lives for some weeks in complete darkness, it may happen that the neuronal sensibility of the visual process in the brain evolves to such an extent that he or she can start to consciously see objects by the rays of subtle matter emitted by his or her eyes. Such an ability to see in the dark was reported by, among others, the tao-master Matak Chia. In the case of an "extended" or "higher" state of consciousness, the visual process of a person might then be dominated by "subtle-matter cognition", which has been reported to allow the paranormal reading of a newspaper in complete darkness, i.e. in the absence of electromagnetic light.

In 1990 Dean I. Radin, a parapsychology researcher from California, USA, published his research into the effects of looking at different kinds of images (see Fig. 10). His research may help explain our weighing results shown in Fig. 8. In Radin's tests a computer was used to randomly present photos to test participants under standardized conditions. Some pictures, labeled "calm", included landscapes and cheerful people; others labeled "extreme" included violent and erotic topics.

The test subject's Electrodermal Activity (EDA) was continuously recorded throughout the photo presentations. Skin conductance, indicated by EDA, is not under conscious control and therefore is regarded as a tool to measure subconscious emotional reactions. It is often used in lie detectors. The EDA-data of every trial were recorded before, during, and after each image presentation, as an indicator of the emotional state. In total, several hundred such trials were performed.

As can be seen in Fig. 10, calm images typically showed relaxation of the test-subject before, during, and after the target was displayed; thus, no unusual responses occurred. Extreme, i.e. highly emotional, sometimes shocking images, however, caused strong physiological responses, as could be expected.

Fig. 10: Electrodermal changes in persons seeing calm or shocking images

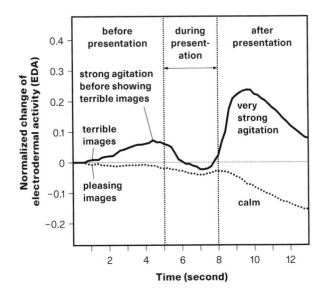

But surprisingly, even before the computer had selected and presented extreme photos, clear physiological responses (Radin used the term "pre-sponse" instead of "re-sponse") peaked on average 1 to 2 seconds before the actual photo was displayed.

This implies that human consciousness received some "precognitive" information about the extreme photos so that it could assess them before selection and presentation. Furthermore, the studies support the idea that people can unconsciously respond to information beyond the reach of normal senses. An explanation of these results is not possible in the modern understanding of physiological and perceptual activities.

From the point of view of a subtle-matter-based science, there are no weighing experiments that directly associated with Radin's tests to date. However, the results of our weighing tests confirm that even all metals carry subtle field-bodies. This implies that technical electronic devices and machines which contain metal parts, may be bound to complex invisible field-structures of subtle matter.

This is expected, for example, in computers, cars, airplanes, ships, heating systems, cell phones, etc. Thus, Radin's computer in his test carried its uniquely individual subtle-matter field with all the qualities characteristic of such fields. The processes in the computer generated the random choice of the photos and this information simultaneously manifested at the level of subtle matter.

Thus, shortly before the presentation of the target photos on the computer screen, there already existed a kind of internal information-processing in the field-body of the computer. These processes in the computer's field-body, and the field-body of the test-persons, might produce some communicative information-exchange. In this manner, without any conscious information via the gross senses of the test-persons, their field-bodies might respond to the information in the field-body of the computer without the person being consciously aware of what is happening. This might explain the observed emotional reactions occurring one to two seconds prior to the visual presentation of the photos on the screen.

This explanation of Radin's results must be tested in future research, but up until now, no other logical explanations for the observed unconscious and precognitive abilities of the human field-body exist, as Radin points out.

In generalizing this result, what happens in the presence of gross systems may have been "prepared" at the level of subtle matter some time prior to its realization on the gross level. This can lead to a fuller understanding of the phenomenon of "time" and of the "time-arrow" in which all gross systems are said to be embedded.

2.3 Subtle Matter and Meditation: Dramatic Weight Changes

Under the theory that visual perception involves two "beams", one of light and one of subtle matter, the subtle-matter radiation from the eye is necessary for an object under observation to register in the consciousness of a human observer.

Likewise, the results of subtle matter experiments indicate that also a weighable "beam of mental attention" (i.e. a "beam of thought") can be sent from the human consciousness to objects of gross matter or living beings in their surroundings. And as many of us who live closely with animals may expect, this proposition probably also holds true for animals.

This may sound strange at first, but many people have experienced that, while sitting in a restaurant or walking through a shopping mall, they suddenly spontaneously turned their head and saw that they were being stared at by another person from behind. From our understanding, this process does not work through electromagnetic light but by rays of subtle matter. This might give an alternative physical explanation to that given by Rupert Sheldrake in his book "The Sense of Being Stared At", 2003.

Certainly, processes like "focusing one's attention on an object", cf. Fig. 8 and Fig. 6, are abilities of human consciousness. The measured weighing effects of such processes give further credit to the hypothesis that human consciousness includes the field-body ("aura") or is interwoven with structures of the field-body that generate the individual's psyche. However, if internal structures of the field-body are inhabited by individual consciousness, then also the total field-body most likely expresses consciousness.

We therefore suggest that the invisible field-body, as the pilot-field of the visible body, represents the human psyche, i.e. the individual consciousness and vital force that pilots the whole. In this view, decision making, for example, may be limited to a degree by other invisible influences from the surroundings. This may be the case with "collective consciousness", which results from the superposition of all individual field-bodies to create a general or holistic subtle field of consciousness with stored collective archetypes (e.g. see C.G. Jung) super-imposed on any social group.

Later on in this book we will see that not only in human societies do such subtle fields of collective consciousness exist, but also in social assemblies of animals or plants.

We will now consider the effects of mental exercises such as meditation on both the subject and his environment, including his social group.

Fig. 11: Weighing test of a meditating person

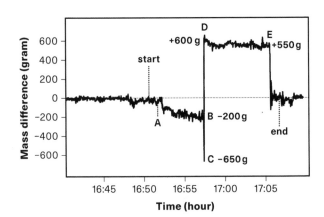

Fig. 11 shows results from a weighing test on the chair-balance with the subject practicing the technique of "Transcendental Meditation®" ("TM®"). Besides a well documented baseline prior to and after the meditation, two highly significant sequential mass deviations occurred in this experiment.

The subject was sitting calmly, cross-legged, without back-rest on the chair-balance. Again the balance was connected to a computer and the weight was measured and recorded every second.

Soon after the start of meditation, a more or less continuous weight drop occurred at time A by about 200 grams which continued until time B. Then followed a sudden negative weight change at C of about −450 grams, giving a total weight loss of the subject from A to C of about 650 grams. From time C an upward weight change of up to +600 grams was measured to time D.

This increase happened in a very short time and since the subject at time C was 650 gram lighter, the jump from C to D shows a total change of 1250 g of weight! From time E, a few minutes before ending the meditation, the weight rapidly dropped back to the baseline-level that was originally measured before the subject started to meditate.

This is a dramatic result, and traditional science is not able to give any explanation for what happened during this silent sitting meditation. Because, for around 7 minutes, the subject's weight remained at about +600 g, it is obvious that the weight jump from position B to C and to D could not have been caused by an involuntary body movement during the meditation session.

At this stage of research into subtle matter these data are not explicable in detail. The question as to why the weight of the meditating person follows these specific changes can only be answered in the future by an extensive research program. Nevertheless these are unexpected and dramatic results and a clear violation of today's scientific knowledge, and they therefore demand further study.

For more clarification about the weight reducing (orderliness-increasing, termed "negentropic" – with positive influence on health) and the weight increasing ("entropic" – orderliness-reducing) effects of subtle matter see the Summary in Section 4.

We will present even more surprising results of further weighing experiments with mental techniques in the following pages.

In an experiment we observed the influence of meditation on a subtle matter roll-detector (8 cm diameter), using a sensitive one-pan semi-micro balance (Sartorius, type RC 210S with a reproducibility of ±10 micrograms), while the meditating person was sitting about 16 feet away from the balance.

Fig. 12 shows the results from the automatic mass difference readings taken from the balance, while a person practiced Transcendental Meditation (TM). First the person was sitting quietly, and then started to practice the meditation. The weighed mass changes deviate very significantly from the independently measured baseline.

In our opinion the automatically monitored highly significant mass changes of the detector show that the decoupled parts of the field-body of the meditator seem to reach and influence the detector in the balance over a distance of about 16 and a half feet. This may also indicate that the subtle human field-body has a spatially extended structure.

Fig. 12: Meditation is influencing a nearby balance

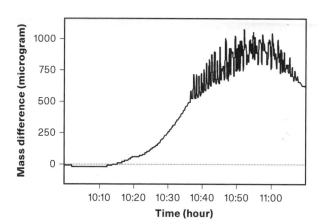

In Fig. 13, the registered mass changes on the side of the roll-detector on the semi-micro one-pan balance are shown. Initially, a meditator was sleeping at a distance of about 16 and a half feet from the balance. After waking, the meditator then practiced Transcendental Meditation at the same location.

In our opinion the significant mass fluctuations indicate quick dynamic emission and absorption, or perhaps rearrangement processes of subtle matter during sleep, but with much higher intensity during the meditation period. Thus, such dynamic subtle processes naturally occur during sleep, but also manifest with much higher intensity during the meditation practice. Since sleeping is generally associated with

43

processes of psychosomatic stabilization and purification, these fluctuations of subtle matter radiation, as registered by the detector in the balance, are apparently intensified during the meditation.

Fig. 13: Weighing tests with a sleeping and then meditating subject

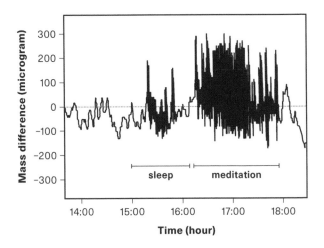

As practitioners of meditation techniques know, many scientific research papers confirm such mental healing processes take place during meditation.

Figs. 11 to 13 show that the technique of Transcendental Meditation yields objectively testable results, both in regard to mass changes of a person's field-body and to subtle matter mass changes in specially prepared detectors. This hints at the possibility of improving human creativity, intelligence, and health due to the deep rest that is gained in meditation.

Fig. 14 shows an interesting detail recorded during the weighing of a person sitting on a chair-balance while practicing the so called "Yogic Flying® technique". Yogic Flying, as taught by Maharishi Mahesh Yogi, is an advanced technique of the Transcendental Meditation program (i.e. part of the so called "TM-Sidhi®" program). In this test the balance had again a reproducibility of ±0.1 gram. The weight of the subject was measured every 0.3 seconds and recorded by computer. A perfect baseline was established while quietly sitting with hands resting on the thighs prior to the beginning this mental levitation technique.

Fig. 14: Dramatic weight change during "Yogic Flying"

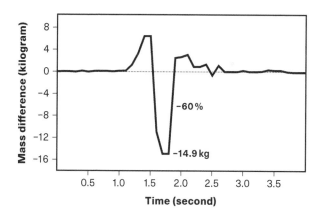

It should be understood that the seating position in this experiment allows muscular body movements only in an upward direction. Such movements would produce an intense increase of weight in an initial peak, followed by oscillating negative and positive peaks each with decreasing intensities until the baseline is again reached.

The peak recorded here, however, does not follow this pattern. As can be seen, only a relatively weak positive first peak (with ca. 5 kg increase) occurred, followed by a significantly stronger negative second peak down to −14.9 kg from the baseline before the weight change of the person after a small, dampened positive third peak returned to the baseline.

A strong body movement, such as hard beating downwards of hands or arms did not happen in this measurement. Therefore the decrease of weight by 14.9 kg cannot be explained as resulting from purely mechanical movements by muscular force. The data indicate that during the subjective exercise of Yogic Flying by the person, a non-classical levitating effect has occurred. It should be understood that the person's body did not completely levitate, but a weight reduction of nearly 15 kilograms nevertheless occurred for a short moment that could not be explained by any well-known forces.

The results therefore demonstrate that levitating effects may really occur during the Yogic Flying program even though in this experiment the effect lasted only for a very short moment. Once again the results of this experiment call for a wide ranging program of weighing research on such techniques for further clarification.

Having seen the effects of mental techniques on both the meditating subject and the detector on a balance some distance away, we then tested the influence of a group of meditating individuals practicing the Yogic Flying on a detector and scale placed in a neighboring room.

Fig. 15: Effect of a group of Yogic Flyers on a balance

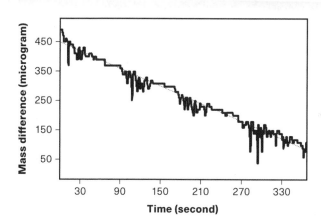

The one-pan balance for this experiment in Fig. 15 was connected to a computer that recorded the weight of the detector every 0.1 second. The apparatus was positioned next door to a group of eight people who performed the Yogic Flying.

The overall decline of the data curve is due to a systematic temperature decrease in the room where the balance was located. It can be seen from the downward sloping curve, which can be understood as a baseline, that associated groups of sudden negative mass deviations occurred.

That these downward directed, i.e. negentropic, weight changes measured at the detector were produced by the Yogic Flyers in the neighboring room is evidenced by the observation that such negative weight changes occurred only during periods when the Yogic Flyers were engaged in correlated, spontaneous "hopping". This emission of negentropic, i.e. life-supporting subtle matter radiation into the surroundings might give a causal explanation to the so called "Maharishi Effect" (see chapter 2.8).

2.4 Subtle Matter Explains Alternative Medicine

So far we have shown strong evidence of the existence of the human subtle field-body and its interaction with the surroundings. These documented results of subtle matter influences during meditation raise more basic questions such as, Can we give scientific evidence of the relationship between health and subtle matter fields, and How far-reaching is the human field-body?

Entanglement of drops of blood: Fig. 16 shows the results of a weighing test with a dried drop of blood on a filter paper in a gas-tight closed glass ampule. Two drops of blood were taken from a sick person by a medical doctor who is specialized in alternative medicine. One drop of dried blood was sent to the laboratory where it was put in a gas tight closed glass ampule and used in the weighing experiment. The other drop of blood remained in the doctor's practice about 400 km away.

The next weighing test was done with the automatic weighing two-pan balance that measured the weight every 10 seconds and stored the data to a computer. At a date and time, unknown at the site of the weighing test, the doctor "treated" the drop of blood, that had remained in his practice, by applying a so called "bio-field-therapy" (see e.g. Wikipedia for "Biofield therapies" or "Energy medicine"). The treatment was done in the same way that this natural cure is applied in naturo-pathy for therapeutic purposes. After this treatment ended, the doctor informed the researcher at the weighing test site about the exact starting and finishing time of his treatment of the drop of blood.

Fig. 16: Entanglement of human blood

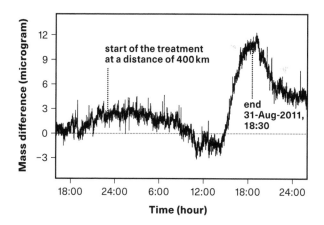

As can be seen from Fig. 16, at the same time as the treatment of the drop of blood occurred in the doctor's practice, a significant weight change of the "twin-blood-drop", was observed in the experiment. The weighing equipment was again, as in all other experiments, thoroughly isolated against any known external influences (see Appendix "Weighing Procedure").

The results raise the question, what could be the reason for the clear weight change at the same moment when the twin-drop was treated over 400 km away? Doesn't this look as if a subtle entanglement between the two subtle field-bodies of the drops of blood was at work?

The present understanding of the properties of subtle matter does not allow us to explain the specific pattern of the obtained weighing curve. Similar tests run concurrently, and a clearer theoretical understanding of subtle matter, are necessary to explain such details. Such entanglements are currently known scientifically only from microscopic quantum mechanical experiments (see https://en.wikipedia.org/wiki/Quantum_entanglement).

Einstein and others considered such behavior to be impossible, and referred to it as "spooky action at a distance". However, modern tests not only confirm the existence of such submicroscopic entanglements, in agreement with theoretical considerations, but also have measured speeds of information exchange between entangled subatomic particles at superluminal velocities to confirm the formalism of quantum theory. The transfer of information between entangled particles may even happen instantly. A mechanism to scientifically explain such quantum entanglements is not known from the accepted scientific theory of today.

The results illustrated in Fig. 16 indicate the following: **First**, even a dried drop of blood has a field-body of subtle matter. **Second**, the spatial extension of such a field-body seems to range over distances of at least 400 km. However, practitioners of the so called "biofield-method" report healing effects over distances of 6,000 km or more. **Third**, our experimental results strongly suggest that the field-bodies of the two dried drops of blood remained entangled, i.e. connected, so that the weight change could occur when only one of the drops was psychically treated.

Furthermore, from the reported healing effects of this kind of complementary medicine, it is plausible that the field-bodies of the two drops of blood also remain entangled with the field-body of the person from whom the drops of blood were taken. This appears to support our understanding that all organs and even cells of the human body carry their own individual field-bodies, and each of these parts contains the total information about the state of health of the body.

Aura Surgery is a rather new technique in alternative medicine. Aura-surgeons claim they can "feel" and remove disturbances and impurities in the aura or field-body of a patient. They also claim to feel, and to be able to remove, "previous life" traumatic experiences. Patients report improvements in high blood pressure, recurring headaches, muscular tensions, or chronic lung problems.

The aura-surgeon "works" with all the traditional surgical instruments, but does not directly touch the body of the patient. The instruments are sometimes manipulated at a short distance from the body, but are moved as if a "normal", surgery is being performed. With diseases of inner organs or the skeleton, the surgeon does the "surgery" with his instruments on anatomical photographs.

Fig. 17: Aura Surgery changes the weight

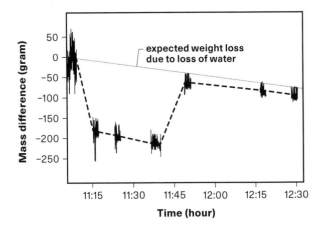

Nevertheless, during such treatments objective mass changes in the range of up to −250 grams were measured over time intervals of 120 seconds each, as can be seen from a weighing test of a patient on a "chair-balance" prior to (first measuring point), and during an aura-surgical treatment, cf. Fig. 17. Mass reductions occurred at the time when the aura-surgeon claimed to remove "dark" parts from the aura.

The highly significant mass changes recorded in this experiment give the first evidential demonstration that aura-surgery, as a purely mental process, seems to be a real treatment of a person's field-body. At the end of the treatment, the subject's weight returns to the expected baseline level with a remaining mass difference of about 25 gram.

Whether or not this mass difference results from some removed entropic (i.e. health damaging) quanta of subtle matter from the patient's field-body is an open question. Similar results to those of this measurement were obtained in sequences of further tests, with observed mass deviations of 1000 grams or more.

Summary: For the first time in history, these measured changes in weight support the conclusion that all forms of life on Earth result from a superposition of an invisible subtle field-body, i.e. the visible body's "life force" or "vital force", bound to the visible physical body.

In all living systems, growth at the microbiological level of the visible physical body is guided in its development and in its internal metabolism from the invisible field-body. This invisible field-body acts as a dominant "pilot-field" and is closely aligned with the consciousness of an individual being. Processes of natural healing generally deal with the field-body.

The Nobel laureate **Erwin Schrödinger** once postulated in his book "What is life?" the existence of a "negentropic action" in living beings. Prior to the experiments described here, little or no experimental evidence of such a negentropic factor existed. This previously unknown factor may now have been found in our research on what we call subtle matter.

Negentropic fourth law of thermodynamics:
The detected negentropic action of subtle matter leads us to formulate an extension of thermodynamics. We propose a negentropic fourth law of thermodynamics that runs counter to the second law of thermodynamics.

The second law states that entropy, i.e. "disorder", always increases in spontaneously changing closed systems. Under the usually low intensity of negentropic subtle global fields, the second law of thermodynamics holds true. But, within high intensity negentropic subtle fields, processes spontaneously start to run in a more orderly way, e.g. by building orderly structures. Until now this has been considered impossible according to the second law.

For more details about the "extension of thermodynamics", including a discussion of the "thermodynamics of irreversible open systems" by the nobel laureate **Ilya Prigogine**, see Appendix 5.3).

In present-day medicine as well as in modern physics, the existence of negentropic subtle actions or the field-body of living beings are unknown and are considered to be non-existent.

Formerly, scientists and philosophers searched for what they termed a "vital force", but without success. This was because the applied experimental methods to find such a "vital force" were insufficiently sensitive.

Currently, the negentropic (Syntropic) "life or vital force" can be detected only by a high-precision, automated weighing, recording, and data processing apparatus. Such equipment has been available only for a few decades.

The individual's field-body as a kind of pilot-field seems to guide the microbiological and psychic processes in every individual from fertilized egg to adulthood. We propose that this information exchange with the physical body happens via field-field-interactions of the field-body and the detailed field-bodies of the structures of DNA, RNA, proteins, fats, sugars, minerals, vitamins, trace elements, cells, and cell organelles etc.

It is general knowledge that the physical body, as a physical system, needs regular input of ordinary physical gaseous, liquid, and solid components, through breathing, drinking and eating. However, from our new understanding, the human field-body also requires "subtle food" on a regular basis as a kind of nourishment. The field-body takes its subtle food from the field-bodies that are usually bound to fresh food or to fresh healthy water, and maybe to gaseous molecules in the air we breathe.

In principle, these field-field interactions of the human field-body with external subtle fields can be called, in the case of consumption of food, for example, "plant-field/human body-field interactions" to remind us of the importance of the subtle quality of our food. This understanding can give a new, causal interpretation of complementary medicine, alternative medicine, energy medicine, integrated medicine, or holistic medicine etc.

If our interpretation of the above experiments is correct, besides the gross components of food, clearly, subtle field-components of food are extremely vital for human health. Thus it will be worth introducing research on these subtle qualities into academic education at universities. These studies should also cover the knowledge of paranormal states of consciousness, their potential for diagnosis, and new possibilities for individual and collective health.

Not only must the discipline of medicine be extended (i.e. we may term this discipline "biogene biology") but also the discipline of biology, because all living beings appear to be carriers of individual field-bodies.

Finally, in principle, also so-called "lifeless objects", such as rocks, metals, minerals and gemstones as well as negentropic-field loaded plants and water, etc, belong to a previously unknown biological discipline we may call **"abiotic biology"**.

It seems that in the case of human beings, the ability to extend consciousness towards more and more refinement and conscious perception of subtle/gross resonances is highly developed. On the other hand, in animals, plants or rocks (or even celestial bodies) the degree of conscious resonance, i.e. expression and practical use of subtle effects, decreases systematically.

Nevertheless, when we consider what may be added by this new dimension of subtle matter, a rock, a million year old quartz crystal, a tree, the oceans, or a celestial object may have a highly evolved form of consciousness, endowed with many paranormal abilities and great intelligence and wisdom.

But there is still another class of objects, i.e. man-made machines, equipment or, for example, electronic devices. These kinds of equipment also are carriers of their own subtle field-bodies. Thus, a self-sufficient creative intelligence may well develop in sufficiently complex, non-linear electronic circuits.

It is possible that "machine-fields" may develop in "artificial intelligence" (including the worldwide web, i.e. the internet) through their ability to memorize and to learn how to handle subtle information in addition to their handling of ordinary information.

Of course considerations of **abiotic biology** and **artificial intelligence** may be challenging for the reader, and possibly with good reason. Such "inanimate" machines possibly fall far short of the capabilities inherent in the complexity of humans and probably not even the complexity of animals and plants. What we have outlined above nevertheless opens new areas for consideration in the proven reality of Nature, and widens the possible significance of our research into Subtle Matter.

Individual Health, Individual Diseases and Complementary Medicine:
A person's subtle pilot-field must be understood, then, as existing permanently under the influence of the competitive effects of negentropically and entropically acting fields, as well as under the influence of grosser levels of the environment. In this respect, some further components seem to be crucial for the question of the development of human health or illness:

First, how much is Rupert Sheldrake's global morphic field involved, which, from our understanding, is acting negentropically, i.e. in a health improving manner?

Second, people's own individual paradigm of reality, and especially all the subtle collective consciousness fields where people live, have a major influence.

Third, subtle influences of buildings are likely of great importance.

Fourth, "Electrosmog" is another factor whose burden on human health is becoming more apparent. In view of all these influences, suitable plant-field/body-field interactions may possibly help to overcome chronic disease and other health blockages arising from such influences, see Appendix 5.5. This hypothesis is supported by research into medicinal plant preparations as applied to chronic diseases, cf. Nederlands Tijdschrift voor Geneeskunde 5 (33), 586–594 (1989).

Historical Considerations:

It is important to note that, since ancient times, intuitive people in altered states of consciousness have recognized that there is something more to life than just the visible physical parts. Around 400 B.C. the Greek philosopher **Democritus** proclaimed that there are two forms of matter. One form should constitute the World of visible objects, each of which, if divided more and more, should finally yield indivisible constituents, i.e. present-day atoms and elementary particles. The other form, Democritus stated, being invisible, should be involved in the area of emotions and consciousness, and if repeatedly divided, it should also finally result in indivisible components, which we might now term the quanta of subtle matter.

In ancient forms of medicine, such as in Chinese traditional medicine, vital force was termed "qi", "Chi" or "psi". In Indian Ayurveda, a subtle field recognized as "Veda", is the invisible, yet real, basis of the visible physical World. The non-linear behavior of Veda was cognized and described in detail by people in higher states of consciousness. The aspect of Veda which is especially involved with the field-bodies of living beings was termed "Soma".

Modern medicine, following the understanding of modern physics, has dealt mainly with the gross body of humans. Modern medicine attempts to explain consciousness as an entity emerging from neurological physical network-processes in the gross brain. Our results documenting the existence of subtle matter offer a paradigm extension to modern medicine. Clearly, the possibility that the human (subtle) field-body is the primordial negentropic basis of life should be thoroughly investigated by modern medicine.

2.5 Does the Subtle Matter Field-Body Direct Your Brain?

As mentioned, modern mainstream neuroscience tries to explain human consciousness as emerging from the processes of neuronal networks in the human brain. Present-day science is convinced that, from the Big-Bang-origin of the Universe to the brain of human beings, anything must be explainable from a purely materialistic point of view.

According to our data on the subtle matter effects in connection with the human body (the "hardware"), the brain and body are just resonance instruments of the corresponding subtle pilot-field. It is our proposal that this field represents, or is close to, individual consciousness. It might be thought of as the system's software, which guides and controls the visible body and expresses itself through it.

Although this proposal is based on our research in subtle matter fields, it is conceivable that this relationship between body and the subtle pilot-field is equivalent to the historical relationship of the body to the soul – where the soul is using the body as its vehicle.

This implies that decision making, for example, does not take place in the electromagnetic neuronal processes of the brain, but in the body's subtle pilot-field. This is where the ego, the thinking processes of the mind and intellect, and the long-term memory of a person are all located. This understanding is consistent with the statement of the famous consciousness scientist **Stanislav Grof** who says that the brain is simply a reducing valve, or an interface to the mind, which is located outside of the brain.

Also sensory perception has its basis at the level of the field-body, as some of the experiments described earlier seem to show. These hypotheses are further supported by the reported observations of people after near-death-experiences (NDE) or out-of-body-experiences (OBE) (see Section 2.11). In such cases, subjects have reported the complete and total conscious experience of their own individual existence without a gross brain or body.

Human Existence without Brain?

The hypothesis that the human brain is only a resonance instrument to the individual's subtle brain as a subsystem of the field-body is further supported from the observation that man can live a near normal life with no, or almost no, physical brain.

In 1980 **John Lorber** studied the autopsy results of several people who died from unusual diseases and reported that only 1% or less of their cerebral cortex remained. The intelligence quotient of one of these individuals had been determined in his lifetime to be above 120. Another of the persons concerned had been a mathematician. In everyday life of these people, no neurological deficits at all were observed.

In another case, reported by Christoph Wilhelm Hufeland, again due to a rare disease, no brain at all could be found during the autopsy, although when alive the individual had shown no neurological deficits. No explanations exist for such cases in modern medicine.

In a recently published case, a patient who, in 1980 had contracted severe meningitis, lost the parts of his brain cortex which were considered as the critical and sole substrates for "interoceptive awareness", i.e. the ability to have self-awareness. Nevertheless, this patient showed all the signs of self-awareness (see Nature Neuroscience 12, 1494–1496, 2009), even though the brain areas thought to be required only contained an aqueous liquid.

Based on such findings, neuroscientists are beginning to discuss the possibility that other neuronal areas are responsible for self-awareness. As already mentioned, such observations give credence to the hypothesis that the gross human brain is only a resonance instrument responding to the field-body where both the psyche and self-awareness reside.

The Neurological Binding Problem (BP):
The "binding problem" considers how the brain assembles or segregates various elements of sensory input to enable recognition of discrete "objects". This is termed

the "segregation problem" (BP1). In other words, when looking at a blue square and a yellow circle, what neural mechanisms ensure that the square is perceived as blue and the circle as yellow? Another form of the binding problem is how objects, background, and abstract or emotional features are combined into a single experience. This is termed the "combination problem" (BP2). The binding problems are one of the greatest unsolved mysteries in neuroscience.

No direct experimental findings from weighing experiments yet exist in this regard (except for the results depicted in Fig. 8), but the recognized existence of the subtle brain as a subsystem of the field-body may be of major importance in explaining the BP1 and BP2 processes. This hypothesis must be tested in future research.

Phantom pain:

Phantom pain involves the sensation of pain in a part of the gross body that has been removed. The neurologist **V. S. Ramachandran** reports in his book "Phantoms in the Brain" about a test with a person, named John, who had lost his right arm: "I placed a coffee cup in front of John and asked him to grasp it [with his phantom limb]. Just as he was reaching out for it, I yanked away the cup. He cried "Ow!" and yelled "Don't do that!" "What's the matter?" he was asked. "Don't do that", he repeated. "I had just got my fingers around the cup handle when you pushed it. That really hurts!"

Ramachandran's interpretation of this event was that the phantom fingers which had gripped the cup were certainly illusory, but the pain was real. Indeed, the phantom pain was intense enough that Ramachandran didn't dare to repeat the experiment. This test-result confirms our statement that the gross limbs of a person are only following the subtle limbs of the field-body, and that subtle limbs still exist and react even after the loss of a gross limb. Furthermore, this test appears to imply that pain in general is felt only in the field-body, not at the level of the gross body.

Does the human Body carry further Forms of subtle Matter? There may be other forms of what might be called subtle matter than those we have detected from their weighable macroscopic mass. Seers from the ancient Vedic tradition say that about 120 such invisible types of increasingly finer forms of subtle matter exist. Naturally, from a scientific point of view, this hypothesis needs confirmation in further research.

2.6   Group Field-Bodies and Collective Consciousness

As already mentioned, when people live together, congregate, or work together for some time, their individual conscious field-bodies start to overlap and generate a "subtle group-body", i.e. a "group-field", that is superimposed on the individuals as a form of "group" or "collective consciousness", see Fig. 18. Such collective fields should not be confused with the global negentropic morphic field, where primordial information regarding human beings and all other living entities is stored. Collective consciousness is, so to speak, "man-made", and reflects archetypical thinking and behavior of the group-members. It may change over time, but this is a slow process.

Fig. 18: Sketch of a collective group-field

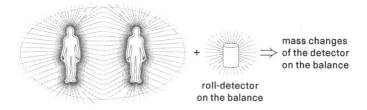

roll-detector
on the balance

mass changes
of the detector
on the balance

In principle, the existence of such group-fields can be tested by weighing experiments. An appropriate experimental setup with the semi-micro one-pan balance is depicted in Fig. 18. Group interactions may affect weight changes of a nearby detector. It is proposed that the detector's subtle matter field-body can interact with a group-field if the intensity of the group field is strong enough. This may yield mass deviations of the detector according to the internal dynamics of the group-field consciousness.

In these next two experiments, Figs. 19 and 20, we show weighing results produced by the semi-micro one-pan balance with automatic PC-data-recording. Initially, a horizontal baseline was established, without subtracting the value of the first data-point, by weighing a reference sample over a period of 6 hours, see the baseline at the bottom of Fig. 19. This showed that the balance worked properly under normal conditions. Then the reference sample was replaced by a roll-detector (see Section 4.4, Detectors for Subtle Matter) and was weighed during a 12-person seminar coffee break. In this situation the detector showed strong random mass-fluctuations which indicated that the individuals were operating more as separate beings, not in a collectively coherent state. However these fluctuations were on a significantly higher level from the negligible mass fluctuations during the baseline test with the brass-sample (the almost flat line at the bottom of the graph).

Fig. 19: Subtle matter effects from the collective consciousness

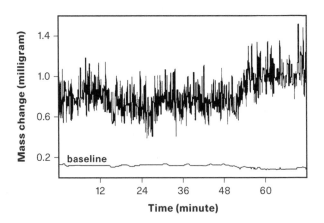

Similar mass variations of the detector also were recorded during a music concert break attended by about a hundred people. This strongly suggests that the collective consciousness of the group was influencing the weight of the detector even though there was no physical contact between any member of the group and the balance.

Fig. 20: More effects from the collective consciousness

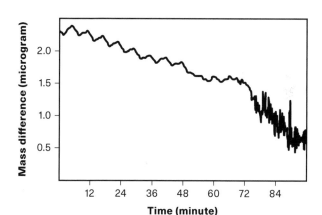

Weighing results of the next experiment, recorded during a 10-person seminar, are shown in Fig. 20. First, the leader of the seminar gave an overview of the goals of the seminar in general terms. This report was easy for the participants to follow in a relaxed mood. Over a period of about 50 min, the detector showed a harmonious oscillation. The average linear drop of the data was due to a systematic temperature change in the room. The curve during this time can be interpreted as showing an oscillating, attentive and settled, collective participant group-field.

The lecturer then presented a concentrated series of mentally demanding technical details. At this time the mass difference curve changes and shows a typical noise-pattern, due to the individuals' independently focused attention and loss of the coherent group-field. These weighing results appear to indicate the existence of "collective group-consciousness", i.e. "subtle group-field", as its own entity of consciousness, although these data represent only the start of such studies. Further development of this weighing method should shed light on a likely fruitful and important area of research into the social effects of "subtle collective group-fields" in various areas of society.

From these types of studies, it may be found that any association of people in companies or families builds up such fields. Also, the people in villages, towns, cities, regions, states and continents all may have a subtle pilot-group-field, respectively, guiding their population's general patterns of behavior, belief, thinking, speech, etc.

The importance of such studies is obvious, because decision makers are clearly no longer independent individuals but are influenced by ideas that arise in a group-dynamical process at the level of the subtle collective group-consciousness. As mentioned, also nations have a pilot-group-field, and the more negentropically (harmonic) integrated a nation's pilot group-field, the better public welfare will be within the country. The global subtle field-body of the Earth may relate to Rupert Sheldrake's morphic fields and probably also to the effects of Nelson's Global Consciousness Project (GCP).

The "Maharishi Effect":

Neither modern psychology nor modern medicine yet recognize that the psychic abilities of every individual around the World are always interacting on many levels with each other and also with the various universal fields. This is going on, whether people meditate or not and whether they believe in such effects or not. Everyone reflects, according to his or her individual abilities, a more or less large or small fraction of the universal subtle fields.

We are unconsciously connected to collective subtle fields at various levels and also to what can be called universal creative "field-libraries" of a living Universe, with higher, more universal subtle entities.

Modern science has yet to discover that through systematically increasing the subtle field-field resonance of an individual's field-body, to global and cosmic field-entities, human awareness can rise to "states of higher consciousness". Such states seem to be difficult or impossible to achieve by intellectual or emotional efforts. Consistent application of a technique which provides the ability to effortlessly transcend subtle levels of human existence, makes it possible to merge closer and closer to the universal fields of existence.

One way to achieve this is through the practice of Transcendental Meditation (TM) from Maharishi

Mahesh Yogi. However there are other techniques from which to choose.

Our research suggests that collective consciousness exists, and may be proven by specially designed weighing experiments, developed from those shown in Fig. 19, 20, at the same time but at different places. For example a setup could be designed where, during the time of a group meditation, weighing experiments are performed at different distances and locations to evaluate the far reaching effects of the meditation. Collective consciousness can be seen as a kind of agreement in the brains of people about what is accepted as reasonable in society. We pointed out that collective consciousness is of utmost importance for societal human health.

This is because there is an ongoing competition in collective consciousness, for example of a nation, between the sum of peaceful (negentropic) feelings and actions of people, and the sum of negative or destructive actions. This implies that collective consciousness may "fall sick" if it gets entropically dominated. In this case nations (or other groups like families, companies, regions or the whole world) may be disrupted, for instance, in man-made economic, enviromental, political, terroristic or even military conflicts.

Are there treatments to "cure entropically loaded (disorderly, inharmonious and chaotic) social collective consciousness"?

It appears that such man-made consciousness (or subtle matter field) effects can be overcome by groups of human beings practicing the required technologies together. We believe that group collective consciousness can be purified from stored entropic tendencies if large groups of meditators regularly practice together. The negentropic qualities produced in their individual consciousnesses thus "injected" into the greater field must result in harmonization of collective consciousness as a whole. Such an effect was predicted by Maharishi Mahesh Yogi in the early 1960s.

During the 1970s through 1995 when large group-meditations took place, statistical analyses of social tendencies in various areas of the World gave clear evidence for the effect. From the statistical results it could be deduced that such a harmonizing social effect became detectable if the number of participants in such groups of meditators was greater than 1% of the total population. This effect was termed **"Maharishi-Effect"**.

A further hypothesis was that the application of the advanced meditation practice, called "TM-Sidhi®" program, including "Yogic Flying®", should greatly increase the negentropic efficiency of meditating groups to produce the Maharishi-Effect. This expectation was confirmed in other large assemblies of TM-Sidhi trained meditators. Research showed that a group of such meditators need only be greater in number than the square root of one percent of the population to produce an effect equivalent to 1% practicing the TM-Sidhi program separately. This improved effect was termed the **"Extended Maharishi-Effect"**.

Finally, scientific studies on this phenomenon have repeatedly demonstrated that a group of at least

7,000 individuals practicing their TM-Sidhi program with Yogic Flying together in one place on a regular basis can produce this coherence-creating effect on a global scale, reducing violent and negative trends worldwide and yielding an increase in positive social, economic, and political trends. This effect was termed **"Global Maharishi-Effect"**.

To sum up, the TM- and TM-Sidhi programs of Maharishi Mahesh Yogi offer simple mental techniques to reduce the present entropic political or, for example, social and economic effects in collective consciousness in all countries. Not only individual human health could be improved in society but positive trends in other areas of life should also rise significantly through the application of these consciousness based technologies.

Of course, it would be helpful if similar research into the effects of large assemblies of people under other circumstances could be done, to see whether similar results can be achieved independently. For the first time our research into subtle matter provides a physical explanation for all such collective effects.

Fig. 21 shows, the crime rate variation during a long-term test of the Maharishi-Effect in metropolitan Merseyside, England. In March 1988 the crime rate in Merseyside suddenly dropped down from being in third place in the English crime ratings list to having the lowest crime rate of any metropolitan area in England. This was due to the Maharishi Effect achieved when the number of participants in collective, twice-daily practice of the TM- and TM-Sidhi programs became sufficiently large.

Fig. 21: Changes in monthly crime rates

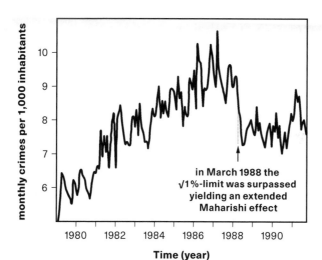

Subsequent research has confirmed the existence and the universality of the Maharishi Effect. The TM-Sidhi program was practiced in large groups on numerous occasions in different countries in the 1980s. A first statistical analysis of the effects of social harmonization was published in 1987. The results showed for example a decrease of about 11 % in violent crimes in Washington D.C., in total crimes in Metro Manila, and in total crime in the Union Territory of Delhi. The p values (the probabilities p of the observed changes happening by chance) of these effects were $p < 0.01$, 0.005, and 0.001, which are excellent for any study in social science.

73

It became possible to lodge a prediction in advance with the police and the mayor of a city and then create the effects. This was put to the test under the scrutiny of a distinguished review board in 1993 in Washington D. C., where a reduction of crime of 20 % was predicted. The measured maximum decrease in violent crimes was 23.3 % (see Pearson, C., "The Complete Book of Yogic Flying", Maharishi International Press, 2008, or Hagelin, J., et al., Social Indicators Research 47, 153–201, 1999).

Even though the statistical significance of the results in studying the Extended Maharishi Effect was very high, questions were raised regarding the existence of a causal connection between an assembly of meditators and social effects of collective consciousness. As already mentioned, results of weighing tests as described above may be helpful in this regard, see Fig. 15 and 21.

2.7 Altered States of Human Consciousness

On the basis of the subtle matter research described thus far, we will expand our discussion regarding some psychic phenomena that are known from "parapsychology". We touched on some of these areas in the preceding text.

Visual perception:
As we have seen, recent subtle matter evidence indicates the visual physiology of men and animals works as a "two-stage subtle/gross process". Modern physics agrees that the well known form of "gross electromagnetic ra-

diation" is emitted or reflected by an object under observation. Our research shows that another kind of "subtle non-electromagnetic radiation" is crucial to the visual process. This subtle radiation is emitted from the eye, and is simultaneously reflected from the object of attention.

Evidence suggests that only when both the subtle and the gross rays reach the eye and are neurophysiologically processed in the brain does the object become consciously "seen" by an observer. If one of the two rays is missing, the observer falls blind. The non-electromagnetic ray, emitted as a kind of "Beam of Sight" from the eyes, as Plato and Epicur stated, was detected in several of our weighing experiments (see Fig. 5). However, as we all know from experience, in the usual waking state of consciousness, visual sight is dominated by the electromagnetic processes, and only gross objects are seen. The ability to "see" subtle fields, such as auras, is sufficiently developed only in a small number of people, even though everyone has the latent ability to achieve this.

The human field-body has been described phenomenologically by various paranormal gifted persons (see, for example, C. W. Leadbeater, Man Visible and Invisible, 1900, or Dora van Gelder Kunz, The Chakras and the Human Energy Fields, 1989). But only systematic high precision weighing experiments such as those described in this book have given objective proof of the existence of the invisible subtle human field-body.

There have been reports, however, that the neuronal sensitivity of the brain of a person who lives for some weeks in complete darkness, may increase to such an extent that the person starts to "see", in addition to the gross objects in his or her environment, also the subtle fields. Thus, a person may start to perceive the spatially extended subtle "aura-field" of another person. In this case the usual waking state has evolved to an "extended state of altered consciousness". Persons in such states usually are referred to as being clairvoyant.

Clairvoyance and remote viewing:
Many people in history report experiences indicating they were endowed with clairvoyance. They report things such as having conscious cognition over large distances or within microscopic areas, perhaps by using the non-electromagnetic component of light or beam emitted from the human eyes.

How could **Democritus**, for example, come to the conclusion that visible matter is built of atomic and indivisible particles? If this was not a purely speculative statement on his part, it seems that an evolved clairvoyant can "zoom in" (by "micro-psi") from the macroscopic level of the visible associations of gross matter to their microscopic primordial entities. Similar abilities can be deduced from the reports of **Charles W. Leadbeater** (see Stephen M. Phillips, Extrasensory Perception of the Subatomic Particles, Journal of Scientific Exploration 9 (4), pp. 489–525, 1995).

On the other hand, how could Democritus find out that besides the visible form of matter another type of matter invisible to the eye exists that also has an atomic and indivisible nature and is basic to consciousness?

Again, if this was not a purely speculative statement of his, we must conclude that Democritus had clairvoyant abilities that enabled him to recognize subtle matter, its structures, and its functions. As a result of our research, we now believe clairvoyance is a latent ability in every human being. The "atomic" nature of subtle matter was also described by **Gottfried Leibniz** (and others) and the respective particles were termed by him as "monads". However, this does not mean that Leibniz's "Monadology" directly corresponds to our understanding of subtle matter (see Wikipedia for "Monadology"). These may be partially or fully distinct entities.

In 1759, **Emanuel Swedenborg**, was in Gothenburg which is about 300 miles from Stockholm. He cognized a fire breaking out in Stockholm and described the event in detail. Only a few days later, the details were confirmed when a messenger arrived from Stockholm.

We feel that the experimental results shown in Fig. 5, 6 (Beam of sight and thought) give a previously missing, causal physical explanation for this well documented event, and for clairvoyance generally. The experimental results of Fig. 5, 6 reveal that, in the process of seeing, every human being (or animal with visual abilities) is unconsciously emitting a beam of subtle matter from cells in the retina. This beam is neuropysiologically registered after its reflection from an object under observation, together with the electromagnetic light which is also reflected from the same object.

And, as we have seen, if either of the two forms of reflected radiations is missing, a person falls blind. In paranormally extended states of consciousness of human beings, not only does the visual effect of electromagnetic light and structures become visible, but also the subtle structures and effects in the near and far surroundings.

We propose that every human being has the latent ability to develop clairvoyance, and that this holds also for the other paranormal capabilities. Thus, Swedenborg appeared to have lived in such a state of "extended consciousness" that allowed him to see subtle fields, even to "zoom out" over a distance of about 300 miles.

This implies that clairvoyants can use the visual non-electromagnetic component of perception not just for "zooming in" to the realm of microscopic areas (see "Clairvoyance" by C. W. Leadbeater) but also for "zooming out" over large distances, which is termed "remote viewing" or "remote perception".

"Zener Cards" and remote Viewing:
Unlike common playing cards, Zener cards have only five figures. They were first introduced into parapsychological studies of "extrasensory perception" (ESP) by Karl Zener in the 1930s. In a standard test of clairvoyance, the experimenter randomly takes a card, keeps it hidden, and then the subject tries to "remotely view" the card. If, after a large number of trials, the person scores about 20 % more correct guesses than

would be expected by random chance, he or she is considered to have psychic ability.

Joseph B. Rhine used this test extensively in his extra-sensory-perception (ESP) experiments. He claimed that special test-persons scored between 39.6 % and 100 % correct. Rhine's results have never been duplicated by scientists, even though many studies were done at various universities. Perhaps weighing tests could be used to select persons with unusual, i.e. paranormal, mental abilities to reproduce Rhine's results successfully.

Clairvoyance and Psychokinesis (PK):
From 1979 through 2007 a great number of tests regarding remote viewing and psychokinesis (PK) were conducted by **Robert G. Jahn** and **Brenda Dunne** at Princeton Engineering Anomalies Research Lab (PEAR).

The basis of their technique was to rigorously apply statistical methods for data-evaluation. In studying human/machine anomalies they used, for example, a "Random Mechanical Cascade apparatus" (RMC). If metal balls were dropped from above through this apparatus as expected from empirical chance distribution they should assemble at the bottom of the apparatus in a row of compartments in the form of a Gaussian curve.

Hundreds of trials were performed where a person looked at the falling balls with the intention that they should shift either to one or the other side. Such shifts could be found by a statistical analysis that identifies a smaller second maximum besides the main distribution maximum. This was interpreted by the PEAR-researchers as proof of a successful anomalous, i.e. paranormal, psychokinetic interaction.

Research in subtle matter may yield a causal explanation for the PEAR-experiments.

First, experiments have found that in the process of visual perception, the human eyes emit a beam of non-electromagnetic radiation with macroscopic mass.

Second, it was found that during focused mental intention a similar beam of thought can be mentally emitted to a physical object, see Fig. 6, and **third**, this kind of subtle matter radiation exchanges gross momentum with normal matter in scattering processes.

This implies that the subtle beams of radiation emitted from the people in the tests with the Random Mechanical Cascade apparatus at PEAR, could influence the falling balls in such a way that the balls were to some extent pushed to the side that the person intended. This causal explanation may bring the PEAR-results into the realm of science, as opposed to pseudo-science, even though independent reproductions of the experiments are still missing.

Telepathy:
The results of Fig. 6 show that human beings are, in principle, able to intentionally emit a mental beam of thought of non-electromagnetic nature, and to focus it on any object. Similarly, it should be possible to send such a beam to another person.

Subtle mental information transfer between two persons depends on the mental and neuronal abilities and sensitivities of both the transmitter and the recipient to subtle matter fields. If the sensitivities of both persons are acute enough, they will produce subtle matter field resonance, i.e. telepathic field-field resonance. As described above, when discussing clairvoyance, there may be no spatial restrictions for such telepathic communications, and as we will see later, such communications may travel with velocities much greater than the speed of light, because such telepathic processes work at the superluminal 8-dimensional level.

The laws of special and general relativity (SR & GR) are not violated by the above because they are relevant only to the 4-dimensional level of gross matter.

Precognition:

In Fig. 10, results of tests were presented suggesting that the subtle matter field-body of humans has the ability to unconsciously communicate with the complex internal processes of a computer's own field-body. At the field-level, information is exchanged a short time before images are displayed at the gross-level on the computer screen.

To generalize, **first**, events at the gross-level originate from electromagnetically and non-electromagnetically invisible processes that occur before the manifested event takes place in our (gross) visible World.

Second, if the mental sensitivity of a person is sufficiently evolved, he or she may become able to "see", in a precognitive subtle field-field manner, what may happen in the future.

From this scenario results a further consequence that commonly is regarded scientifically as impossible. But the fact may be, that anything that has already happened to a person in our visible World, was "prepared" in field-field interactions by the person himself or herself in the past, maybe in the present lifetime or in earlier lifetimes.

This scenario is confirmed by famous mediums such as **Edgar Cayce, Nostradamus, Helena Blavatsky** and many others. Edgar Cayce obviously had the mental ability to turn his mind away from the visible 4-dimensional gross World, and to tune it into the invisible, yet real, 8-dimensional level of the subtle World of subtle matter field-field processes. He has been called the "sleeping prophet" because he did this while resting on a couch like a sleeping person.

During more than 40 years of his adult life, Cayce gave a total of 14,306 psychic readings and, in an unconscious state, answered questions that had been put to him, by speaking out diagnoses of illnesses or making prophecies about events yet to come with a certain chance.

Psychokinesis (PK):
From the results of Figs. 8 and 6 it can be seen, that, through mental processes levitational psychokinetic effects can be produced, and the results can be objectively detected in weighing experiments.

In Fig. 8 the mental intention of the person being weighed on the chair-balance was focused on several external objects, yielding mass changes of the person him or herself.

In Fig. 6 the focused mental intention was directed from a person to an external object being weighed on the two-pan balance, yielding a reduction of the object's weight. In both cases the focused mental intention may have caused an increase of intensity of a subtle negentropic field, thus yielding an anti-gravitational lifting effect. In both cases the psychokinetic effects apparently were not achieved by a new force but by altered gravitational effects produced by varying intensities of negentropic fields of subtle matter.

If the "sender" becomes identical to the "object" upon which the sender is "charging" negentropic or entropic subtle field-energy (see Fig. 8) a person should be capable, in principle, to levitate up and down through the air, while directing such levitation and or horizontal movements in any desired direction.

Psi-Tracks and Dowsing:
In 1987, Swedish parapsychological experiments suggested that when a person, i.e. the sender, concentrates vividly on a physical object in his surroundings, a "psi-track" (i.e. beam of thought) seems to be established to the object. This track can be detected by dowsing while circling around the sender. When the dowser gets the usual reaction from his dowsing-rod, the spot is marked. If increasingly larger circles are made, a se-

quence of spots will be found which point in the direction of the object on which the sender was focusing his attention.

Systematic research in Sweden and Germany confirmed the effect. This indicates that human thought and directed attention leaves a detectable impression in our surroundings.

It is of interest to note that by dowsing, the existence and spatial extension of the human field-body can be detected. This phenomenological recognition supports the following explanation of the psi-track effect.

From the results of Fig. 6, it is known that by focusing the intention on an object, a mental subtle beam of non-electromagnetic radiation is sent to the object. By reflection of this beam from the object a kind of standing wave is established between the sender and the object.

Because our research has shown that subtle-matter fields can interact with each other, this standing wave should be detectable by a dowser from a field-field interaction. This field-field interaction may act at the dowsing-rod. The fact that the psi-track, when established, persists for some time, even after the sender has left his place, indicates that a kind of "carrier" for the psi-track must exist. The role of such a carrier may be filled by the global subtle field-body of the Earth, which may be also the basis of Sheldrake's subtle morphic field or of the subtle Hartmann-grid.

Levitation:

Levitation in the paranormal context is the raising of a human body into the air by mystical means. Some parapsychology and religious believers interpret instances of levitation as the result of supernatural action of psychic power or spiritual energy. In cultures and ancient traditions across the globe, levitation effects are known. The scientific community states there is no evidence that levitation exists, and that levitation events are explained by natural causes such as "magic trickery, illusion, and hallucination".

As in all areas of life, trickery and deception may play a role also in alleged levitation events, and many "levitating mediums" have been shown to be frauds that are using stage magic tricks that were later exposed.

In 1868 **Daniel Dunglas Home**, for example, is reported to have levitated on one occasion, out of the third floor window of one room of a house and back in through the window of the adjoining room, in front of three witnesses. In 1920 some skeptical researchers exposed the "levitation" of Home as nothing more than him moving across a connecting ledge between two iron balconies, see Joseph McCabe, "Is Spiritualism based on Fraud? – The Evidence Given by Sir A. C. Doyle and Others Drastically Examined", Watts & Co publishers, 1920, pp. 48–50, or Trevor H. Hall in F. B. Smith "The Enigma of Daniel Home: Medium or Fraud?", Victorian Studies, Volume 29, No. 4, pp. 613–614, 1986). Did the three witnesses to Home's levitational "flight" in 1868, not have a look outside the window to see the ledge between the two balconies over which Home must have been passing safely within a few seconds?

Nevertheless, there exist reports about levitational events that are beyond doubt. From **Joseph of Cupertino** (1603–1663), for example. In the official biography of the Saint, which was first published in 1767, the author states that: *"Not only during the sixteen years of the Saint's stay at Grottella, but during his whole life, these ecstasies and flights were so frequent, as attested in the acts of the Process of Beatification, that for more than thirty-five years his superiors would not permit him to take part in the exercises in the choir and the refectory or in processions, lest he disturb the community."*

In the records of his process of beatification, seventy of his levitations and ecstatic flights are listed, and many healing events. St. Joseph was often enraptured into remarkable levitations, often being carried away for some distances.

One Christmas Eve the Saint invited some shepherds to join in celebrating the birth of the Savior. When they started to play bagpipes and flutes, the Saint let out a cry of joy and flew a considerable distance through the air to the high altar. He remained there in his rapture about a quarter of an hour. Many witnesses attested under oath to St. Joseph's levitations, among them persons of high standing such as Princess Maria of Savoy and John II Casimir Vasa, King of Poland and Grand Duke of Lithuania.

From the perspective of subtle matter theory, human levitation is possible and is explainable. The brain and body are able to increase the intensity of the negentropic subtle component, by interacting with the "omnipresent" negentropic global field, to such an extent that the anti-gravitational force overcompensates the gravitational attraction of the physical gross body. Such anti-gravitational subtle effects have been measured in weighing experiments (see Fig. 14).

Apparitional Experiences and Progress of Life after Death:

Apparitional experience is an anomalous, quasi-perceptual experience. It is characterized by the apparent perception of either a living being or an inanimate object without there being any material stimulus for such a perception.

Phenomena of these experiences are often attributed to "ghosts" and are usually encountered in places a deceased individual is thought to have frequented, or in association with the person's former belongings. If a living person has achieved a sufficient sensibility to consciously cognize subtle field-structures, he or she can "see and/or feel" the subtle 8-dimensional field-entities of deceased people. But if such a person has no intellectual understanding of his or her abilities or of the reality of a "living field-body" of a deceased person, usually a heavy shock results.

When leaving the physical body irreversibly in death, the main factor that determines the further steps and progress of the field-body, i.e. the primordial "field-entity", also known as his or her immortal "life-force", "vital-force", or "individual consciousness", is guided by his or her own paradigm, established during the just completed lifetime in our visible, gross World.

These paradigmatic imaginations of one's own "paradigmatic reality" yield resonance-processes after death to other invisible "field-structures" and "field-entities" that also do not possess a physical body, and that have similar imaginations of "reality".

Normally, the field-entity of a deceased individual leaves the Earth after death of the physical body and should mentally move to various celestial areas in the Solar System. "Travelling" through universal space is in such a case no problem, and works with superluminal velocity. The proper functioning of the field-body is maintained automatically by a permanent flow of cosmic negentropic subtle energy through it, which is independent of where the field-body is. This flow of negentropic subtle energy through the body is, even in physical life on Earth, a prerequisite for a healthy life. Sometimes people try to exist only on this flow of subtle negentropic energy.

This is called "living on [subtle, negentropic] light" or "living on prana". Such "living on light" was demonstrated by Saints, for example, by the national Saint of Switzerland, **Niklaus von Flüe**. If this support of the physical body by the field-body does not work, death is unavoidable.

People who have no idea at all that they survive death with their field-body, and firmly believe in their paradigmatic (likely materialistic or physicalist) kind of reality, may after death roam about as invisible field-entities for some time here on Earth, usually in the local environment where they had been living.

2.8 Ancient Knowledge About Subtle Matter

It is interesting that the emergence of paranormal human abilities and methods to gain knowledge about subtle effects are independent of any present-day high-tech inventions or technologies. Already the ancient cultures of Sumer, Babylon, India, China, Egypt, Polynesia, or Greece, for example, had gained knowledge of Nature and its invisible microscopic physical components as well as its invisible subtle background.

Such ancient information may be worth studying also from a modern scientific point of view. The particle accelerators of many wise people in ancient traditions of knowledge were their evolved brains in higher states of consciousness.

In ancient Greek schools of knowledge, subtle matter and its basis were described by various philosophers. Anoxagoras spoke about the cosmic level of the "Nous", a "universal mind", which from our understanding is the all-pervading subtle cosmic field. As already mentioned, Plato reported the existence of a kind of invisible primordial matter. Aristotle described a kind of *"materia prima"*, and defined it as an invisible "life force" or "entelechy", the qualities of which are quite close to our findings regarding negentropic subtle quanta and fields.

Fig. 22: Some persons who described aspects of subtle reality

| Anaxagoras | Democritus | Plato | Aristotle |

| Nikola Tesla | Viktor Schauberger | David Bohm | Rupert Sheldrake |

Democritus also declared the existence of two forms of matter, a visible one which generates the gross objects in the Universe, and an invisible (subtle) one, as the origin of consciousness. Both forms should finally become indivisible, i.e. "atomos", if continuously divided.

In ancient India the subtle reality was termed "Veda", in China "Qi" or "PSI". The Dalai Lama quotes from ancient Tibetan wisdom about a form of "space-like matter" from which everything in the Universe is emerging. In Australia "Dreamtime" is an ancient Aboriginal concept of "time out of time". In the Middle Ages, Crescas cognized subtle realms. Later, in Europe, Giordano Bruno and Leibniz spoke about "monads" (i.e. likely quanta of subtle matter).

In modern times subtle matter was obviously involved in the research of Freiherr von Reichenbach and Emanuel Swedenborg. Nikola Tesla reported about non-classical free energy generation (maybe, from subtle matter). Viktor Schauberger started to technically apply principles of subtle matter in water vortices (see Fig. 30, 31). Pfeiffer, Kolisko, Schwenk, and Kirlian developed subtle test-devices. Erwin László defined a "fifth field" (perhaps subtle matter). Hartmann detected a subtle global grid, and Rupert Sheldrake described phenomenologically the global morphic resonance and a global morphic field. Leadbeater and Emoto spoke and wrote about subtle phenomena that may connect with subtle matter.

David Bohm formulated an interpretation of quantum mechanics, based on hidden variables which fits excellently to actions of subtle matter. He described two levels: an "implicate (i.e. subtle) order" and an "explicate (i.e. gross) order".

Masters of Knowledge:
Nevertheless, all this, and much more knowledge was recognized by other ancient seers over thousands of years and is still stored today in some form not widely recognized in today's science, perhaps such as Sheldrake's morphic field of the Earth. From time to time persons can raise their consciousness to such an extent that they can clearly cognize this universal knowledge as easily as if they would visit a library. Commonly, such persons are termed "Masters".

Usually, their teaching is focused on invisible, yet primordially important aspects of life. Such Masters recommend technologies to turn the mind inwards, away from the visible World to increase by mental processes, i.e. "meditation", the individual's resonance to the invisible fields of nature. Such Masters sometimes take a great risk in teaching their understanding, as can be seen from the lives of Socrates, Jesus Christ, or Giordano Bruno (who cognized that the Universe is a cosmic being, a highly creative and powerful universal subtle creature, but it seems he did not realize in his paranormal view the negentropic cosmic field of consciousness at the basis of subtle matter), and others.

The structure of the "**Veda**", as a subsystem of the invisible, yet real parallel subtle Universe, was first described in detail by the ancient Vedic sage Vyasa, also called Veda Vyasa.

Patanjali's "Yoga Sutras":
One of the great authorities of ancient knowledge was the Indian Yogi Patanjali. In 1955, Stephen M. Phillips published a paper on "Extrasensory Perception of Subatomic Particles" in the Journal of Scientific Exploration, Vol. 9, No. 4, pp. 489–525. In his paper he describes eight psychic powers, or "sidhis", as originally described by Patanjali (c. 400 B.C.) in his "Yoga Sutras".

Among these sidhi-powers are abilities a yogi can acquire, such as "knowledge about the small (i.e. "micro-psi"), the hidden, or the distant by directing the light of a supernatural faculty", (meaning possibly by directing the mental and visual beams of non-electro-magnetic radiation, see Fig. 6), on objects, for example, in remote viewing. Another sidhi-power described by Patanjali is levitation. However, all these abilities can be of practical use in human life only if the physical brain of a person is evolved enough to consciously and actively realize subtle field-field interactions in an altered state of consciousness.

Another such Master in our time was **Maharishi Mahesh Yogi**, who taught the same Vedic knowledge of an invisible, yet highly creative universal subtle field of consciousness termed the **Atman**. The Atman can be understood as a higher dimensional consciousness, a Cosmic Self. The Veda can be activated for personal and for collective use, by meditation technologies.

Maharishi cognized the Veda as "total knowledge", as the "total field of natural law", as the blueprint or "Constitution of the (visible) Universe". Additionally he regarded every human body as an "embodiment of Veda" and thus as an "embodiment of total natural law".

As already mentioned, the meditation Maharishi offered is termed Transcendental Mediation (TM). In this form of meditation, the wakeful human mind transcends all levels of mental activity and finally merges into a field of cosmic consciousness which physically is the basis of all existence. Seen from the practitioner's point of view, this implies that in practicing this meditation his or her mind transcends levels of intellect, emotions at the subtle level, the world of visible physical objects including local or universal subtle fields and then experiences the field of pure unbounded consciousness.

Fig. 23: Modern Masters of Vedic Knowledge

Maharishi Mahesh Yogi   Dr. Tony Nader

Today, TM is classified as one of the many aspects of alternative medicine. Maharishi's TM-Sidhi technologies of consciousness are based on the ancient knowledge of Patanjali (see above). The results of our objective and reproducible weighing experiments presented in Figs. 11 through 13 show that the TM- and the TM-Sidhi programs produce effects through field-field resonance with both global and cosmic fields. Many scientific studies and individual reports support the possible medical, psychic, or social and peace-giving progress of people who practice this easy-to-perform technology.

In 2000, Maharishi honored **Dr. Tony Nader** as his successor. Maharishi charged Dr. Nader with the responsibility to achieve and maintain permanent World Peace (https://en.wikipedia.org/wiki/Tony_Nader). Dr. Nader is the author of the books "Human Physiology: Expression of Veda and Vedic Literature" and "Ramayan In Human Physiology", and is the founder of a new "Veda-based Medicine". Further research in subtle matter may find that the above described human field-body of subtle matter may be identical to the individual's local aspect of the Veda as described by Dr. Nader.

2.9 The Soul of Plants and Animals?

It is interesting to look at the research of **Theodor Schwenk**, a German scientist who was born in 1910 and worked most of his life for the anthroposophic company Weleda where he was engaged, amongst other things, in water research. During the solar eclipse of July 1st 1954, he conducted a set of experiments to investigate the influence of the event on the growth rate of wheat seeds.

Besides simply studying the effect of the eclipse, he also experimented with what he termed "potentiated" water. The test tubes of water were shaken prior to, during, and after the eclipse, in sequence every 15 minutes and then stored. After the shaking of all the test tubes, he placed wheat seeds into them, and, in the following days measured the growth-rates of the seedlings. The results are shown above in Fig. 24.

Clearly, the sprouts showed a significant reduction of growth rate during the solar-eclipse, as compared to the growth rates obtained before and after the event.

In our view, these results indicate that during the solar eclipse an increased quantity of entropic subtle

matter, emitted from the Sun and focussed gravitationally by the Moon's field-body was absorbed into the
shaken, i.e. "potentiated", water and produced growth-
destroying effects in the sprouting seeds

Fig. 24: Reduced seed growth rate during solar eclipse

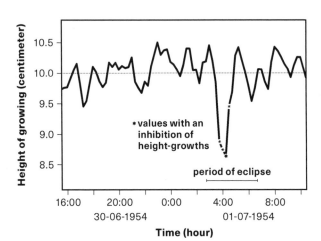

Schwenk's study gives support to the historical idea
that celestial bodies like the Sun radiate subtle matter as well as visible light. We conducted extensive
research to check this hypothesis with weighing experiments during special alignments of constellations, the
Sun, Moon, and specific stars (see chapter 3 ff.).

Maria Thun, (1922–2012) devoted her entire research
career to investigating how the positions of the Moon
and the planets influence agricultural success. She
became one of the leading authorities on biodynam-
ics and her annual "Biodynamic Sowing and Planting

Calendar" was regarded as an essential agricultural almanac.

Both Theodor Schwenk and Maria Thun were inspired by the Austrian philosopher **Rudolf Steiner** who is also well known as the founder of the Waldorf Schools which can now be found all over the world.

In 1924, Rudolf Steiner outlined the principles of biodynamic agriculture. He spoke of subtle life forces that are not detectable by the human senses (in the waking state), yet which link together the Universe and all living beings. He postulated that the energy of living systems is affected by the energy (most likely the subtle matter fields) of the Sun, Moon, planets, and stars and suggested that the decision about when to sow or to harvest should be made according to the most auspicious astrological positioning of constellations and planets.

From her investigations Maria Thun reported similar effects to those of Theodor Schwenk. Over a period of more than 50 years she planted and irrigated seeds under the influence of solar eclipses and studied the growth rates of the seedlings. She came to the conclusion that seeds planted during a solar eclipse start growing normally, as they would during normal solar conditions. However, after about two weeks, a significant majority of the plants started to die suddenly.

We would explain such changes in growth rates under cosmic influences as being caused by interactions of the various far-reaching subtle matter fields of the Sun, the Moon, or solar Planets with the phase boundaries of the water-based plant systems. Our research indicates that celestial bodies each have their own subtle matter field-bodies and that stars are permanently emitting entropic and negentropic subtle radiations besides their known forms of radiation. This gives credit to the teleological, i.e. astrological, entanglement of living systems on Earth with celestial bodies of the solar system and even beyond.

Erwin Bünning (1906–1990) was a German biology researcher and professor who is considered to be the discoverer of the "inner clock" of plants (later giving rise to "chronobiology", the science of circadian and other biological rhythms).

Both Schwenk and Thun's results can be understood in the light of subtle matter research. Fig. 25 shows some research results by Bünning regarding the sprouting-rates of straw-foxglove (digitalis lutea) seeds over the course of a year.

The upper dot-dash curve in Fig. 25 shows the normal sprouting rate of untreated straw-foxglove seeds. In winter the sprouting rate was close to 100 %. It dropped down to values of about 75 % in midsummer. This can be understood as due to variations of the entropic and/or negentropic solar subtle field radiation in different seasons. The other solid curve shows the sprouting rate of straw-foxglove seeds that were heated at 110 °C for two minutes before their use in the test. In winter times these thermally treated seeds showed a sprouting rate of 0 %.

In other words, because of the thermal treatment, they had died off, probably due to thermally damaged

DNA-strands, denatured proteins, or damaged mem-branes etc. But in midsummer, their sprouting rates reached values that are more or less identical to those of the undamaged seeds.

Fig. 25: Subtle matter from the Sun "repairs" damaged seeds

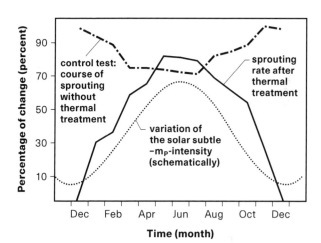

This shows that the increased levels of negentropic, life supporting solar radiation during midsummer had the capacity to regenerate the thermally damaged seeds.

These results confirm that any increased intensity of negentropic subtle matter acts in a regenerative way on biological systems – an effect that can also be used in complementary medicine. Furthermore, these results indicate that plants (as well as animals or human beings) all have their own, bound, individual fields of subtle matter that are influenced by interaction with the solar subtle fields.

Rudolf Hauschka (1891–1969), an anthroposophical chemist and inventor, was the founder of "Wala Heilmittel" which still produces the well-known "Dr. Hauschka" range of skin care and cosmetic products based on his research. His work takes into account rhythmic processes found in nature. Rudolf Steiner influenced him greatly and anthroposophical medicine became his methodological approach to the study of nature, medicine, plants, and natural phenomena.

It was encouraging for us, regarding our weighing research, to discover that around 1934 Hauschka himself had the idea to experiment with the long-term accurate weighing of sprouting seeds. He intended to study the influence of the Moon and other celestial constellations on growth rates.

Hauschka in 1934 used mechanical balances comparing pairs of airtight sealed glass ampules. The sample ampule contained some cress seeds together with some water and air. The reference ampule, initially the same weight as the sample ampule, only contained water and air.

He conducted two sets of weighing tests per month over a year. The first test period started about 3 to 4 days prior to a full moon and continued for about two weeks until the sprouts had died due to lack of oxygen.

The second test period started about 3 to 4 days prior to the following new moon. In the tests starting prior to full moon (see the curves in the left column in Fig. 26) Hauschka's results show significant mass increases of the sprouting seeds.

Fig. 26: The Moon's influence on sprouting seeds

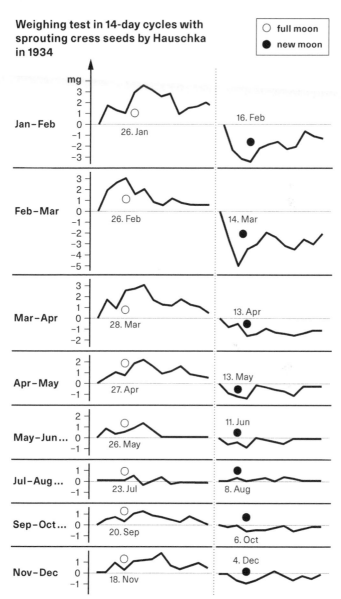

Weighing test in 14-day cycles with sprouting cress seeds by Hauschka in 1934

○ full moon
● new moon

The full moon period mass increases he discovered were significantly higher during the first half of the year (spring and summer), than in the second (autumn and winter). In contrast, all but one (August) of the new moon test periods produced significant mass decreases in the sample.

In both cases, midsummer sample mass deviations, were reduced. The reasons for this diminished effect, and other inexplicable results, are so far unknown. In this regard we should remember that subtle matter-fields are not only bound to the Moon, but also to the Sun and other more distant celestial bodies. It is likely that the surprising weight changes found in these studies could be explained if the detailed interaction of these subtle matter fields from different sources were known.

Let's remember that, as in our own weighing experiments, Hauschka was using airtight sealed glass tubes! From the traditional scientific understanding, due to the law of conservation of mass, the weight of the tubes should never change!

The weight changes therefore can be expected to result from a previously unknown, subtle and invisible form of mass which is able to penetrate the glass of the sealed tubes.

After studying Rudolf Hauschka's work, we conducted several tests to try to reproduce his results with modern weighing technologies using a Mettler mechanical balance with an accuracy of plus or minus 0.1 milligram.

Fig. 27: Reproduction of the experiments of Hauschka

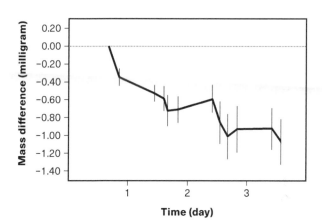

Fig. 27 shows the results of a weighing experiment which was conducted April, 30th of 1985 with 95 % error bars. We recorded, the mass deviations of sprouting Mung Beans in sealed gastight 250 ml glass flasks as compared to empty gastight sealed flasks over a period of several days. A mechanical balance manufactured by Mettler, with a weighing reproducibility of plus or minus 0.1 mg, was used. The test and reference samples were weighed several times per day. The oxygen content within each flask was sufficient for the sprouting seeds to survive for several days.

According to the law of conservation of mass it is impossible that a sealed flask containing seeds, water, and air can change weight over time, even if the seeds sprout! And yet, it happened again in our experiment as was already found by Hauschka.

The highly significant weight reduction depicted in Fig. 27 indicates a systematic, strong negentropic influence on the sprouting seeds. This confirms the findings of Hauschka and, once again, proves the existence of a subtle field-body with real mass in living-systems.

We ran several experiments simultaneously to ensure that the test samples were fully protected and there were no artifact influences on the results. We monitored temperature variation in the surroundings, air pressure changes, and electromagnetic fields, all of which showed no influence on our results.

The moment "life" manifests in the seeds at the beginning of sprouting, subtle matter enters the seeds by binding to the newly formed phase boundaries of the fresh growing cell membranes and initiates the growth of the plants, as indicated by our recorded weight changes. In Hauschka's tests, after a few days of growth, the seedlings died off, due to lack of oxygen contained in his closed ampoules. The moment the seedlings die off, their earlier mass deviations return to zero, i.e. the field-body is emitted in the dying process.

This confirms that, what is understood as a "living system" is a composite structure of two components, a gross, visible one, and a subtle, invisible component.

Gross life starts when an adequate, more or less complex association of quanta of subtle matter enters in a fertilized seed, and at death gross life ends when such an association of field-like subtle matter separates from the visible gross body (see the following Fig. 28).

Biologists consider that the gross bodies of plants or animals are exclusively essential for life. Based on our research, we would say that the invisible vital force of the field-body is at least as essential, if not even more important for the continuity of life. A negentropically dominated subtle-matter field-body is the basis of health, and allows any disorder in the system of every individual to be regenerated under the right conditions.

The field-bodies of living beings are influenced by the cosmic background radiation of subtle matter. Thus, there is a teleological cosmic connection between every living being on Earth and the Universe.

This is the basic assumption of the field of astrology recognized for several thousands of years in human cultures, where persons with paranormal abilities have subjectively recognized such a connection. Our weighing tests presented in this book appear to verify this cosmic connection as a reality, while modern science denies such effects.

Every subsystem in living beings carries its own individual field of subtle matter, a "smaller field-body", so to say. This holds also for a single leaf of a tree or a bush, or a blade of grass. Fig. 28 shows the last two hours of a continuous weight measurement recorded after a freshly gathered lilac leaf was sealed into a gas tight closed glass ampule. The first 14 hours are not shown in the graph because the weight did not change during that time.

But the last two hours can be interpreted to show the loss of the leaf's field-body at the "moment of death" (due to the depletion of water and oxygen), and finally the emission of the leaf's field-body, constituted of negentropic subtle matter, through the glass wall of the ampule. These changes are indicated by the mass change steps that occurred over a period of about 5 minutes, as shown in Fig. 28.

Fig. 28: Weight jumps of a dying lilac leaf

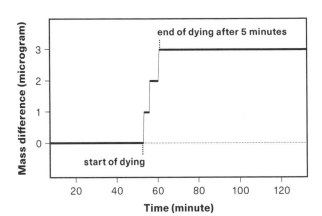

The lilac leaf was fresh and green prior to being sealed into the ampule, i.e. in a good state of health, so its field-body must have been negentropically dominated.

Let's remember that our research revealed that negentropic subtle matter shows a life supporting and weight reducing quality (one could say the subtle negentropic field-body seems to be more "ethereal" and thereby lighter). Thus, when the field-body left the (now dead) leaf, a mass-increase was observed, i.e. the leaf got heavier not lighter as normally might be expected.

Whereas in the case of beings dying from severe illnesses, their field-bodies will be entropically dominated, and therefore their weight can be expected to decrease when the field-body leaves the gross body.

Regarding this, it is interesting to note that in 1907, a Dr. MacDougal at a clinic in Boston, MA, USA, recorded mass losses of up to about 40 grams in patients who died of tuberculosis (which was incurable, due to the lack of antibiotics at that time). The patients themselves had given permission to the researcher to perform the weighings.

These findings again support our statements about the superimposed gross and subtle structures of living beings. It can be expected that every phase boundary of every sub-system in a living being carries its own individual field of subtle matter, a "smaller field-body", so to say, characteristic for the sub-system but also containing the information of the total system.

The results of the experiments of Fig. 28 show that the bodies of plants are associated with weighable individual field-bodies of subtle matter. The detected field-bodies of human beings, animals, and plants are invisible, yet they possess macroscopic mass, energy, and information content. A question arises as to which if any human qualities can also be attributed to the field-bodies of other living entities?

For instance, do plants have emotions or memory, do plants feel pain or have any kind of perception? Do plants experience thoughts?

In 2003, **Cleve Backster** from USA published positive answers to such questions in his book "Primary Perception: Biocommunication with Plants, Living Foods, and Human Cells". **Jagadish C. Bose**, who was an Indian scientist, had demonstrated a similar principle in the early part of the 20th century, claiming that plants can feel pain and understand emotional affections.

In 1966 Backster attached polygraph electrodes, a part of a lie-detector, to a Dracaena plant, to measure galvanic skin responses (GSR), attempting to determine the time taken for water to reach the leaves after watering the roots. Astonishingly, the readings he recorded closely resembled those of humans. This made Backster try different scenarios. Thus, he immersed, for example, the end of a leaf, which was neighboring the measured leaf, into a cup of hot water. But no noticeable chart reaction occurred.

However, to his surprise, the GSR meter registered his mentally intended threat to burn the plant by getting a match and to burn the plant's measured leaf. Not only had the plant demonstrated fear, and thus emotions, it might also have "read" Backster's mind, and thus had shown extrasensory perception.

Backster also showed with his experiments that plants have memory and could recognize special human individuals who had damaged or killed other plants or even living cells in front of them. He discovered that distance was not important and electromagnetic shielding also made no difference.

Modern science rejected Backster's findings because of the difficulty of their repeatability. It turned out that purely intellectual approaches to replicate such "psychic reactions" of plants failed. This led to an important observation about the challenges of using the scientific method to test consciousness.

This is because the plants had the ability to distinguish, for example, between real intent and just faking it. In addition, the plants tested by Backster had the ability to change their response and to learn, so that a process that worked once to elicit a response from living organisms or cells would not necessarily work again.

Thus, researcher intent and subjective subtle abilities as well as the plant's subjective attitudes can play a decisive role in the outcome of experiments in testing consciousness. Therefore, in research into subtle forms of consciousness, the current scientific principles of reductionism and reproducibility are no longer adequate.

On the one hand, skeptical researchers may apply experimental scenarios to study "consciousness of plants" which may convincingly and consistently confirm their prediction that no such consciousness exists because plants may have "decided" not to react at all in their tests.

On the other hand researchers whose field-body would come into positive resonance with the field-bodies of the tested plants could come to the opposite conclusions, with their own convincing and consistent results. So both standpoints can be made consistent to themselves.

Field-Field Interactions of Plant Societies with the human field-body, i.e. "Forest Bathing":

Forest Bathing is a new part of "Nature Therapy". The explanation for the health effects is based on breathing ethereal oils from the trees as a kind of aroma therapy. However another significant health supporting factor may be the subtle field-field resonance between the forest with the field-body of the visitors.

Dermo-optical Perception (DOP):

Anomalous effects exist in human life, and we feel it is worth studying them in detail and without prejudice. One such capability is, for example, "dermo-optical perception" (DOP). It is also known as "eyeless sight", "finger vision", and other names. DOP is not scientifically accepted today. Nevertheless, there are reports about DOP being shown by some definitely blind people.

In 1957, **Ved Mehat**, published his book "Face to Face" where he described in detail how he could bicycle without problems through the crowded streets of his Indian home town even though he had lost his sight from meningitis when he was three years old. He explained this ability as "seeing by his skin".

Viktor Farkas authored a number of books where he documented many cases of DOP. He found cases in which people could "see", for example, via the nose, the ears, the belly, the elbow, the fingertips, or the skin.

The basis for an explanation of these effects may be that DOP occurs via other parts of the field-body than the eyes. As indicated earlier, our subtle matter research leads to the conclusion that human vision requires neuronal processing of the beams of non-electromagnetic subtle radiation, emitted by, and reflected back to, the eyes of an observer, to make the viewed object consciously visible. Even if this process is blocked on the gross level by say, an eye injury, a fully functional subtle brain still exists as a subsystem of the field-body.

If the subtle brain finds another pathway to allow neuronal processing of non-electromagnetic radiation emitted and received, not via the eyes, but from another part of the body, DOP becomes possible. To us, this implies the following **Statement:**

> *"Quanta of subtle matter, and their associations are endowed with all the internal subtle structures necessary for a fully functional living being, including humans. Even a single quanta confers similar psychic abilities to those of humans, on all living beings. However the gross bodies to which such forms of subtle matter may be bound are limited in their capacity to act in the visible World, due to specific psychic and genomic imprinting, effects of collective consciousness and other material conditions and molding factors.*
>
> *During the ontogenesis of a living being the metabolism and morphology of the growing embryo follows the blueprint of its own subtle pilot-field. The development of the pilot-field from the stage of the merging of the field-bodies of the ovum and*

> *the sperm is guided by the variety-specific infor-*
> *mation set "contained" in the global subtle field."*

This implies that also plants may be able to see via their subtle brain, as a subsystem of their field-body, because the human field-body and the field-bodies of plants are built up by similar weighable quanta, or associations of quanta of subtle matter.

Furthermore, this is in agreement with the **"Cambridge Declaration on Consciousness"** of 2012:

> *"The absence of a neocortex does not appear to preclude an organism from experiencing affective states. Convergent evidence indicates that non-human animals have the neuroanatomical, neu-rochemical, and neurophysiological substrates of conscious states along with the capacity to exhibit intentional behaviors.*
>
> *Consequently, the weight of evidence indicates that humans are not unique in possessing the neu-rological substrates that generate consciousness. Non-human animals, including all mammals and birds, and many other creatures, including octo-puses, also possess these neurological substrates."*

Based on our research on subtle matter and the order apparent in subtle bodies, we may hypothesize that all kinds of plants and animals may have, due to their sub-tle field-bodies, equivalent psychic abilities to those of human beings; this may be true even though plants

have neither gross brain nor nervous system comparable to that of humans. However, they may well have
a subtle brain and a subtle nervous system, as subsystems of their subtle matter field-body.

The hypothesis is supported by the above-mentioned
results of Backster or Chandra Bose and also from a
variety of psychically gifted people who have reported
telepathic communication with plants. In telepathic
information exchange with all other living beings (i.e.
by means of the subtle field-bodies) no different "lan-
guages" or "dialects" exist.

Telepathic communication is a universal language.
This implies that telepathic communication also works
between different species of plants, between species of
animals, or between plants and animals (or man). This
universal aspect of telepathy is extensively documented
in the well known book "The Secret Life of Plants" by
Peter Tompkins and Christopher Bird, 1973. They
are not alone. Many other authors can be quoted, for
example, Rupert Sheldrake, Michael J. Roads, Margot
Ruis, or Marko Pogacnik.

This statement asserts that the members of all of
the six biological kingdoms, i.e. of bacteria, proto-
zoa, chromista, plantae (plants), fungi and animalia
(animals and humans), and also viruses or prions, are
to some extent endowed with psychic abilities via their
field-bodies. This can explain why and how Backster
could even make successful experiments with living
microbiological organisms in yoghurt.

Animals:

Animal consciousness has been researched for over 100 years. From the existence of a physical brain and a gross nervous system in animals, it seems obvious that animals must not only have a subtle field-body but are to some extent sentient. Animals can thus experience pain, pleasure, and various other emotions, as is well known. But they also have an intellect to take creative decisions and it is well known that they have memory.

Also animals that have no brain, such as sponges or trichplax, or which possess only a few neurons, as tunicate (for example, sea tulips) or jellyfish, are carriers of subtle field-bodies that are bound by form-specific interaction to their cell-membranes, yielding some psychic abilities. Groups of animals sometimes have extended sensory systems, working on an electromagnetic basis.

Some animals can perceive ultraviolet light (for example, dogs, cats, hedgehogs, reindeer, etc., many birds, some fish and insects), or infrared light (such as snakes), or other animals which hear ultrasound bio-sonar (such as bats or dolphins and whales) or infra-sound (such as elephants) or yet others which follow their way by sensing magnetic fields.

Extensive phenomenological research in extrasensory perception of animals has been performed by **Rupert Sheldrake** and others in great detail. The most concrete explanation of extrasensory perception to date may be given by our research into subtle matter. Extrasensory perception in animals corresponds to paranormal human abilities. As argued earlier in this volume, for the conscious visual recognition of an object both humans and animals require "gross" electromagnetic radiation and directed subtle matter "radiation". While in humans paranormal abilities involving the conscious utilization of non-electromagnetic radiation is not a common skill, in animals this extrasensory perception seems to be wide-spread (see Sheldrake's books "Dogs That Know When Their Owners Are Coming Home" and "The Sixth Sense of Humans and Animals").

A great variety of research into the consciousness of animals is already available. Areas covered include telepathic communication with or among animals (see, for example, books by Penelope Smith, Wolfgang Weirauch, Carol Gurney, Dawn Baumann, Allen Boone and Marta Williams).

In his book on the topic, Viktor Frakas gives an interesting survey of the extrasensory abilities of animals. He also reports how animals have used these abilities in an intelligent way, for instance before earthquakes or other natural catastrophes take place.

Sheldrake reports that in China observations of the unusual behavior of animals is traditionally understood as heralding such events (i.e. on the basis of their subtle ability to preview effects which will take place in the near future).

After accumulated observations of unusual animal behavior prior to some catastrophes in the World even modern science started to investigate the extrasensory abilities of animals. This is surprising, since modern physics has no explanation for the phenomenon, and our subtle matter research is not yet widely known or widely replicated scientifically. The pre-sensing of upcoming earthquakes or other natural catastrophes may be because animals such as rats, for example, seem to register local intensity-changes of the global field which manifest some time before the event.

Collective Consciousness in Animals:
In the discussion of "plant societies" we have understood that the long-distance, subtle field-field-entanglement of field-bodies of plants establishes the existence of collective consciousness among plants.

Collective group consciousness is, so to speak, equipped with all aspects of consciousness, i.e. ego, intellect or decision making, mind, senses, memory, and the ability to communicate, for example. The ability of animals to consciously or unconsciously interact with their variety-specific collective group-field by extrasensory field-field-communication can be seen as the basis of bird flocking, or fish schooling.

"Superorganisms" in Animals:
The outstanding extrasensory powers of insects is another area that may be better understood through knowledge of subtle matter fields. In Fig. 16 it was shown that the subtle field-body of a drop of blood, even after drying, remains entangled with the field-body of the person from whom the drop of blood was taken. Due to this continual entanglement even the actual state of

health of the person can be determined, even when the drop of blood had been taken long before.

Such an entanglement must necessarily exist in groups of living beings. In colonies of termites or ants there must be subtle matter field entanglement between the queen and the thousands or millions of individual termites that all originate from eggs laid by the queen.

Eugène N. Marais, in his book "The Soul of the White Ant", describes his research on South African termites in some detail. The workers and soldiers in such a colony are blind, yet they all fear daylight, except the queen. However the queen of a termite colony is usually confined in a hard-shelled chamber with walls up to several millimeters thick. The queen is much too big and inactive to leave her chamber in which she is almost motionlessly confined. The chamber is perforated by some tiny portholes, giving access to the worker termites that feed and clean her and carry off her eggs to the nurseries, at a rate of about 50,000 per day.

Marais considers a termitary as an "assembled body" with a "group-soul". This is just another expression for a collective "animal society" with an autonomous "collective group-field" having a superimposed subtle field-body. Marais presents arguments that "the workers and the soldiers had to become mere automata governed by the psychological power of the queen. For the same reason, they lost their sight and other senses which are the accompaniment of an individual psyche.

This implies that the field-body of the whole termitary is governed completely by the queen's psyche. She continuously maintains a clairvoyant overview of the whole termitary in all its details, and is creatively planning what is to happen next. This is an extreme expression of an hierarchically structured "subtle superorganism".

Marais describes an experiment which gives credit to this understanding of a termitary: "When a breach is made in a termitary ... the soldiers form a protective circle while the workers repair the breach ... Take a steel plate a few feet wider and higher than the termitary. Drive it vertically right through the centre of the breach you have made so that you divide the wound and the termitary into two separate parts. One section of the community can never be physically in touch with the other and one of the sections will be separated from the queen's cell. The builders on one side of the breach know nothing of those on the other side. In spite of this the termites build a similar arch or tower on each side of the plate. When eventually you withdraw the plate, the two halves match perfectly after the division cut has been repaired.

We cannot escape the ultimate conclusion that somewhere there is a preconceived plan that the termites merely execute. From where does each worker obtain his part of the overall design? While the termites are carrying on their work of restoration on either side of the steel plate, dig a furrow enabling you to reach the queen's cell, disturbing the nest as little as possible.

Expose the queen and destroy her. Immediately the whole community ceases to work on either side of the plate. We can separate the termites from the queen for months by means of this plate, yet in spite of that they continue working systematically while she is alive in her cell; destroy or remove her, however, and their activity ceases.

Marais concludes, that it is a "psychological power", not just pheromones, which guides the work of the termites because, when the queen is destroyed, "immediately" all work in the termitary stops, not only the repair work on both sides of the steel plate.

Naturally, we conclude, that at some level the same factors that drive the collective superorganism of a termitary are responsible for producing the swarming of birds or the schooling of fish. The reason given for the termite's subordination to the "swarm-intelligence", i.e. the collective intelligence guided by the queen, is that this behavior gives a higher chance of survival to the termitary. Similar behavior has been detected in social communities of ants.

There is yet another extrasensory capability of a termitary queen worth noting. As the queen grows, she has to change her hard walled chamber about six times and move into a larger one, prepared by workers beside the existing chamber. The details of the move from the old to the new chamber are unclear. On the one hand, the queen is unable to move, and on the other hand she would not fit through the chamber's tiny portholes even if she could move. Marais describes this problem in a termitary clearly and in all details, without proposing any solution.

A similar problem of the queen's moves in nests of atta ants was studied by **Ivan Sanderson**. In his book "Animal Treasure", 1938: regarding this kind of Leaf-Cutting ant colony and their queen "It has been observed that, if you do get to a queen chamber and carefully slice a side off it, you may observe the tight fitting insect within and can mark it carefully with a squirt of dye. As long as the chamber is left open, or resealed only by a piece of glass, nothing happens. Often the queen dies or is taken apart by the workers, sometimes she just goes on egg-laying, dye and all.

However, if you cover her up even for a few minutes, something happens. She vanishes! ... Further digging in some colonies of ants within hours of covering the queen, brought to light, to the astonishment of everybody, apparently the same queen, all duly dyed with intricate identifying marks, dozens of feet away in another super-concrete-hard cell, happily eating, excreting and producing eggs!" Sanderson continued to expound a belief that atta-queens travelled from chamber to chamber by paranormal "teleportation", a term coined by Charles Fort. And this may also be the solution to the queen's move in a termitary.

However, the hypothesis of such a teleportative move is so startling that it has not yet reached serious scientific exploration, even though similar effects have been observed occasionally with humans, birds, or fish (see the books by Viktor Farkas).

We conclude these considerations with the remark that Nature has apparently given humans no exclusivity in regard to using psychic abilities based in subtle matter. In principle, we are shifting the complex control mechanisms of the microbiological metabolism of humans, animals, and plants from the gross physiological level to the subtle non-linear field-bodies of these beings. The extraordinarily complex metabolisms of living beings must be considered as mere expressions of the field-body's metabolic information processing. From this it becomes obvious how complex and hierarchically structured the internal dynamics of non-linear subtle field-bodies, and of quanta of subtle matter must be.

2.10   Subtle Matter in Water

Gerald H. Pollack a professor at the University of Washington in Seattle has postulated a fourth phase of water in addition to the commonly known phases, liquid, solid ice, and gas. His formal name for this fourth phase is exclusion-zone water, i.e. EZ water (see Gerald H. Pollack, "The Fourth Phase of Water", 2013).

What he found is that negatively charged "exclusion zones" are arranged in layers of several hundred micrometers thickness in which the water molecules form highly organized laminar structures. These structures differ significantly from the structures found in the other three phases of water.

These exclusion zones show special physical properties, such as electric charge separation or dynamic transport of liquids in thin pipes where EZ-water is present.

Such effects can contribute, for example, to the rising of water in trees from the roots to the leaves inside the so-called xylem tissues. Modern science has yet to explain how trees can transport water to their top leaves in apparent contradiction to all known scientific laws.

Fig. 29: Highly ordered, crystalline-like layers of water

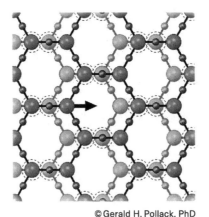

© Gerald H. Pollack, PhD

In our view, such highly ordered phase boundaries are ideal locations for the absorption of subtle matter. Therefore the real basis of the unusual physical properties of EZ-water may be effects arising from EZ-bound subtle-matter fields, especially if this form of subtle matter has a negative sign. Higher intensities of subtle matter in such exclusion zones may play a key role in the dynamical transport of water soluble nutrients from the roots of plants to the highest leaves of trees. A wide area of research is opened here.

Pollack concluded that EZ-water may form fixed layers of EZ-phase-boundaries around all biochemical compounds, such as for example, proteins, cell organelles or DNA in living cells. Because of the dense packing of biomolecules in every cell of a living being, EZ-water likely constitutes the major part of cellular water. The highly ordered EZ-phases around biomolecules are ideal areas where subtle matter can be absorbed to generate local field-bodies. This would allow the embedded biomolecule to be controlled by the internal vibrations of the absorbed subtle field. Thus, from our understanding, EZ-water may play a crucial role in the metabolic control of any gross living body by supporting the formation of a substratum of individual subtle field-bodies.

Viktor Schauberger (1885–1958) was an Austrian researcher who had a deep understanding and appreciation for what he called water's life cycle. He put forth the scientific idea that water is indeed alive, and as such it can be sterile, immature or mature depending on the cluster size, treatment, motion and temperature of the water.

He empirically found that water may have two different forms of flow, yielding water with opposite characteristics. He discovered that one kind of water flow may generate water with life-supporting abilities, while another type appears to deliver water with life-damaging properties. Schauberger claimed that in technical applications where water displacement occurs by screws, for example, water is often generated with life-damaging properties.

Based on this principle, an experiment was designed in our laboratory to combine the Schauberger water vortex and weighing approaches to check for experimental evidence of the observations of Schauberger (see sketch of Fig. 30).

Fig. 30: Water in a Schauberger vortex absorbs subtle matter

funnel with a hyperbolic
shape and with tangential inlet
of the circulating water-flow,
so that a right-turning twist in
the vortex is generated as seen
from a top-position

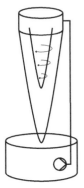

water-tank with an internal
water-circulation pump

The device, as schematically depicted in Fig. 30, was weighed over a period of about 18 hours with the chair-balance having an accuracy of 0.1 g and PC data-recording. The device contained about 5 liters of demineralized water which was permanently circulated at room temperature from a water-container at the bottom of the device via an internally installed pump through a funnel at the top of the device from where the water flowed back to the water-tank at the bottom. The funnel had a hyperbolic shape as described by Schauberger and generated within the funnel a water-vortex with a right-turning twist as seen from above.

During this test the water temperature was measured and remained virtually constant. The whole device was placed in a gas-tight enclosure so that no evaporation was possible. The measured weight results are depicted in Fig. 31.

Fig. 31: Weighing results of a Schauberger-water-vortex

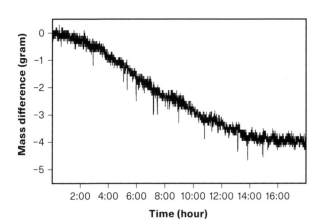

Soon after starting the test the weight of the device started to drop down systematically over a period of about 14 hours, until reaching a stable horizontal plateau of about −4 g at the end of the test.

This second weight-plateau, after about 14 hours of operation, was another proof that the device was really in a gas-tight enclosure. Had the apparatus been open to the atmosphere, the weight would have continued to drop due to an ongoing loss of water by evaporation.

The overall significant weight decrease indicates that subtle matter with a negative sign, i.e. life-supporting and anti-gravitationally acting qualities, had been absorbed within the water. This objectively confirms Schauberger's statement that, through water vortices, a kind of life-supporting negentropic property can arise within the spun water. As Schauberger outlined, this may also happen naturally in river and spring water.

Prior to and after the test, some additional parameters of the demineralized water were measured, such as the values of the water's redox-potential, measured in mV, its pH value, and its electrical conductivity, measured in µS. The redox-potential dropped from an initial value of 0 mV, to values around −50 mV. The pH increased from pH = 7.3 to pH = 8.5. The electric conductivity increased from s = 0 µS to s = 30 µS.

These results indicate further objective effects of subtle matter after being absorbed in water. Once again, these results need to be studied further, and a wide-ranging research program must be undertaken.

Besides this test, further observations reported by other researchers may indicate objective effects of subtle matter after being absorbed in water. Thus, for example, negentropically treated liquid water, from a Schauberger designed water-vortex, produces ice with higher density and hardness than that of normal water.

Present-day science, offers no physical explanations for Viktor Schauberger's research into the health-supporting and health-damaging properties of water arising from its flow-patterns. Schauberger's findings have thus been relegated to the status of pseudoscience. However, the four objective results mentioned above, i.e. weight changes, variations of the redox-potential, changes of the pH, and changes of the electric conductivity of the "spun water", change this situation. Schauberger's "life-supporting and life-damaging kinds of water" are now scientifically explicable due to the actions of the invisible, yet real, negentropic and entropic types of subtle matter being absorbed in water.

More importantly, the possibility of greatly increasing the life supporting "negentropic charge" of subtle matter in water, by the systematic application of water vortices, offers a rich new field of research to confirm the role of subtle matter in water.

"Activation" of drinking Water:

The research, to "activate water", i.e. to give it life- and health-supporting negentropic qualities, has been conducted by many innovative people. Dozens of companies have been founded worldwide, all claiming that they can deliver a form of activated water that supports human health.

Of course, it would be interesting to check all such products in weighing tests or by measuring the other objective parameters given above, especially since there is now a scientific procedure to "separate the wheat from the chaff" in this area.

The human gross-matter body needs gross-matter resources on a daily basis (i.e. nourishment from sugars and starches, fats, proteins, minerals, vitamins etc.). These resources must include sufficient energy content for ATP production to repair and run the gross matter body. On the other hand, the human subtle matter-body also needs a sufficient daily "supply of negentropy", e.g. the negentropic fields provided in fresh food. Negentropically activated water may be another such component of a healthy "natural food supply".

The vortex method of negentropically activating water, as shown in Fig. 30, is probably not the only one. Other approaches and mechanisms to produce enhanced life-supporting water may exist. Of course, the degree of negentropic water "charging" should remain within a life-supporting range (see below).

It would be interesting to compare the different findings of reliable **dowsers** regarding the known qualities of subtle-matter fields in connection with "activated water". The "units" used in this respect in the area of subjective dowsing are usually called **"Bovis units"** ("BU"). Mr. Bovis was a French radiesthesist who first used and defined the units of the "Bovis scale" which is now often used by dowsers and adherents of "geomancy".

According to such dowsers, the healthy human body has about 7,000 to 7,500 BU. Every subsystem, such as organs, muscles, tissues, glands, the nervous system, and so on, carries its own subtle-matter field with its own individual BU-value of about 7,000 BU. This now can be explained, due to the binding of fields of subtle matter to the many phase boundaries in the gross body.

Usually, tap water only registers about 4,000 BU. By drinking tap water at 4,000 BU and daily releasing urine and other excrement at about 7,000 to 7,500 BU, the total negentropic field-intensity obviously drops, i.e. the human gross body gets exhausted and tired.

To remain vital, therefore, the human field-body needs to take in nourishment with increased negentropic subtle matter field-intensities, i.e. with BU-values greater than 7,000. Fresh vegetables and fruits register from 6,500 to 10,000 BU, and are therefore good to eat to maintain vitality. Numbers above 10,000 BU are considered by dowsers, for example, as "Places of Power" on Earth.

The morphology of solid crystal-phases of salts which precipitate from water seems to be influenced by varying intensities of negentropic subtle matter which is bound in the water. This is consistent with the observation of companies who install their devices for "activated water" at household water-supply pipes. They often report that crystallized chalk deposits in the drinking water pipes are reduced by activated water. They also report that in newer pipes with their devices installed, no such deposits occur, even after years.

This suggests that the intensity of negentropic field-loads in water changes the thermodynamically stable phase of crystallization of chalk and may also change its solubility in water. The systematic study of such effects opens another wide range of important research.

Such research could have significant medical consequences, since higher negentropic field intensities in the human body, and especially in the blood vessels, may reduce the risk of plaque deposits on artery and blood vessel walls. Additionally, increased capillary blood circulation could well improve blood and oxygen supply to the whole body. This could also support regeneration after injuries and may reduce the rate of aging.

These considerations, even though obtained from subjective studies, demonstrate the importance of water and its possible "negentropic activation".

From systematic research, more measurable objective parameters will certainly be found in the future. This will give us simple methods to test the "negentropic charge level" in activated water, see the results of Fig. 31. We are confident that small, easy to use devices that monitor this important health parameter in water will become available soon.

Pure and negentropically-activated water can obviously contribute significantly to human fitness and health. Usually "activated water" seems to be loaded with negentropic field-intensities of about 10,000 to 25,000 BU. In the whirled water from Fig. 30 three dowsers determined independently BU-values of up to 15,000,000 BU.

This is much too high for direct use as human drinking water. But such high negentropic field-loadings could be useful in industrial processing plants. Of course, there are probably other methods of producing life-supporting negentropic water, other than by Schauberger's vortex technique. However, any kind of dietary, medical, agricultural, biotechnological, or technical use of the high-intensity negentropic fields of water will need further thorough research and testing.

Negentropically activated water will certainly have further applications other than in being used as a "food supplement" (with BU-values of about 10,000 to 20,000). Such areas will probably include medical care, where healing may be enhanced by using carefully controlled higher subtle field-intensities, or by application of the increased negentropic life force of activated water. Another such area is the generation of so called free energy from the subtle matter field.

Free energy from subtle matter has no climatic or other environmentally negative side effects. Also if the subtle matter field turns out to be identical with the dark matter and energy fields proposed by modern physics, then it may comprise as much as 96 % of the total universal mass. If this is true, subtle energy would be available in omnipresent, inexhaustible abundance.

Various industrial scale technical plants and processes to generate free energy have already been successfully developed. Examples include the production of diesel fuel from water, the production of heat (and thus of electricity via traditional methods), or simply the production of mechanical energy. More such processes will be developed in the near future with the spreading of knowledge about subtle matter fields.

Recently, it became clear to us, that negentropically highly charged water can, under certain conditions, effect the **"transmutation of nuclei"**. This will allow the conversion of chemical elements into other elements, and, moreover, at ambient temperatures and under normal pressures. Currently, with the very low negentropic and entropic intensities available from the two global subtle fields, such nuclear transformations are impossible in bench scale tests under ambient conditions. According to present day physics, very high velocities of electrically charged particles are needed, such as velocities reached in the technologies of CERN or other particle accelerators, to overcome the Coulomb repulsion between two positively charged nuclei to let them merge into each other.

However, in processes with the subtle negentropic Planck-mass, also the very strong Planck-force may be involved so that the weaker Coulomb-barrier between two nuclei may be overcome. This possible effect needs further verification.

Nevertheless, nucleic transmutations have been observed under ambient conditions. Highly increased subtle field-intensities may give us an explanation of transmutations under biological conditions in plants, animals, or even humans, as observed and described, for example, by French scientist **Corentin Louis Kervran** (Biological transmutations, and their applications in chemistry, physics, biology, ecology, medicine, nutrition, agriculture, geology. Swan House Pub. Co. 1972) and others. In healthy living beings the respective subtle field-bodies are negentropically dominated, as we have seen.

Obviously, the body's negentropic intensity can be increased in living beings at the microscopic level by the geometrical spiral structures of proteins or other microbiological macromolecules.

So, for example, the following nuclear chemical transmutative reactions may occur: $Na + H \rightarrow Mg$, $Mg + O \rightarrow Ca$ or $K + H \rightarrow Ca$, as observed by many researchers, but rejected, so far, by modern science. In the process of diesel fuel generation from water by an increased subtle negentropic field-intensity, the following transmutation seems to occur: $H_2O \rightarrow H_2C + He \rightarrow \frac{1}{6} H_{12}C_6$, i.e. liquid hydrocarbon fuel, generated from water. This implies a transmutative decay of oxygen atoms from water into carbon atoms which further associate with the unstable H_2C-intermediates to form liquid diesel fuel.

The branch of physics that is used to describe, for example, spontaneously running processes in nature (such as burning of wood or any fuel with oxygen from air in a flame or fire, a process which spontaneously runs until the wood or fuel is exhausted) is termed "thermodynamics". Closely connected to this topic are special laws of conservation in physics.

As we have reported, most, if not all, such present day known laws of conservation are violated by the effects of high intensity subtle matter fields. Thus violations of the laws of the conservation of mass, of energy (yielding processes which today are regarded as impossible such as "perpetual motion"), or of linear or angular momentum have been experimentally detected.

Also, the forces given by the Coulomb law are overruled, as we have seen in the above transmutation processes. We speculate that this may be effected by the very strong, subtle Planck-force.

This implies that the known laws of thermodynamics need a subtle extension that incorporates negentropic and entropic subtle effects. If the generated subtle fields reach high enough intensities, which today can be generated in bench scale tests as well as in large scale industrial plants or which have been running in biological systems for millions of years, a different kind of thermodynamics may be necessary.

We feel that the most pressing need for an extension of thermodynamics is the introduction of a "thermodynamic law of negentropy". This order generating law exactly mirrors the well known "thermodynamic law of entropy". The current entropy law states that gross processes can run spontaneously only if the disorder (measured by the term "entropy") increases, and under the condition that high subtle matter field-intensities are lacking, as was always the case in the previous centuries of scientific research (for more details about this "extension of thermodynamics", including a discussion of the "thermodynamics of irreversible open systems" by the nobel laureate Prigogine, see Appendix 5.3, Extension of Thermodynamics).

In sharp contrast, the currently unknown "thermodynamic law of negentropy", allows for example, thermally damaged, i.e. by high-entropy, thermally-killed, plant seeds to be revived by negentropic Solar subtle matter radiation, cf. Fig. 25 and 49. Similarly, under the correct negentropic conditions, the process of burning wood with oxygen to water and carbon dioxide can be reversed in a natural spontaneous way. Plants have done this with photosynthesis for millions of years.

Of course, the gross energy needed for this process is coming as electromagnetic light from the Sun. But the entropy-part in this process needs an additional negentropic support from the subtle solar radiation, in analogy to the processes which we have seen in Fig. 25.

This negentropy-component in photosynthesis is so far unknown to present-day physics, even though in 1940, the Nobel laureate Erwin Schrödinger postulated its existence. Now, bench scale tests under increased subtle field-conditions have revealed such negentropic effects.

2.11   Subtle Fields of Life in the Universe

Fig. 32 gives a survey of places in the Universe where invisible subtle matter field-bodies are bound to gross objects by form specific and/or gravitational interaction and places where they play a key role even without being bound to any visible objects.

At the astrophysical level such field-bodies are bound to all gross celestial objects, such as planets, moons, asteroids, stars, galaxies, clusters of galaxies, etc., making them self-conscious living entities.

All living beings carry such life-giving subtle field-bodies, and generate in addition collective field-bodies. In the processes of life and death, all living beings switch back and forth between living 4-dimensional creatures with an 8-dimensional field-body superimposed on a physical body and a condition where these two are irreversibly separated, leaving only the 8-dimensional field-body which has the possibility of being reborn in another physical body.

Fig. 32: Subtle field-bodies are associated with all gross objects

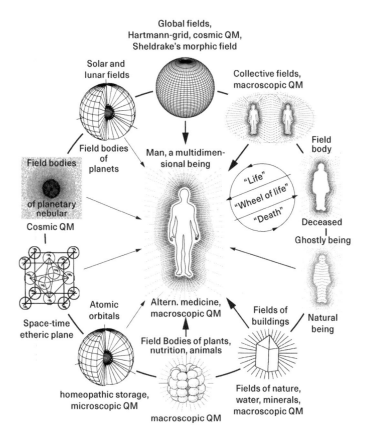

Complex associations of quanta of subtle matter form the field-body of a living or dead person. As already mentioned, this happens in a similar way, as atoms associate to become molecules which then form hierarchical associations of molecules to yield DNA and the whole visible body. This may imply that besides the field-bodies of dead people, also similar invisible individualized field-bodies of non-human, non-animal or non-plant living entities exist in abundance, which never have had, and never will have a visible physical body.

Such "Natural beings" exist, forming a complex hierarchy of "Creatures of Nature" which is integrated, so to speak, with the whole organization of the global biosphere and Universe. Such Natural beings have been known to clairvoyant humans for thousands of years, even though from the perspective of modern science they are considered to be unreal, mythological, or legendary.

People with an evolved consciousness who have developed the faculty of fine perception (i.e. by "field-field interaction") can easily communicate telepathically with such creatures of nature. (See the books of Michael Roads, Margot Ruis, Marko Pogacnik, and many others.) This can further be objectively proven by weighing experiments. In Fig. 33 the results of such a weighing-test are shown.

During the above automated weighing experiment a person with extrasensory perception was weighed on a chair-balance whilehile sitting quietly with eyes open and without any mental intention. A perfect baseline was thereby established. The baseline weight fluctuations recorded the clairvoyant's breathing as expected. This proved that the balance and recording apparatus worked properly. As in all similar tests the reference weight was subtracted from all subsequently detected weights, thus yielding a zero value baseline.

Fig. 33: Weighing the visit of an angel

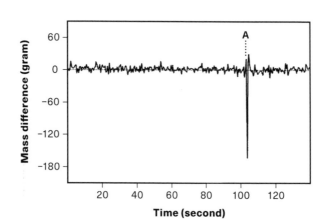

However, at time A the test clairvoyant was mentally asking a Natural being to come join their physical body. At that instant a sudden and significant weight change of about −168 grams of the person's body was recorded.

This result gives credit to the hypothesis that invisible beings exist, that they have real and weighable subtle mass and energy, and that they are able to interact with the field-bodies of human beings. In this case the Natural being's field-body carried weight reducing negentropic subtle matter (i.e. "healthy") and therefore by entering the body of the test person caused a significant weight reduction on the balance.

The fact that the scale did not register intensive upward weight jumps directly before and after the downward jump clearly shows that the mass change did not occur due to a heavy body movement.

In addition, others have claimed that there exist invisible Natural beings without gross bodies who are also endowed with psychic abilities, and who have to perform special tasks in the organization of the biosphere on Earth.

See, for example, the books of **Wolfgang Weirauch** such as "Nature Spirits and What They Say: Interviews with Verena Holstein", where some dozens of Natural beings have been telepathically interviewed, and details of their existence, work, and sorrows with men are described. So, it turns out, that mankind shares "apartment Earth" not only with animals, plants and visible Nature but also with invisible Natural beings.

However, not all such living beings have the capacity to express their psychic abilities like humans or animals at a gross level.

Moreover, clairvoyant persons claim that they can telepathically speak and communicate not only with other human beings, animals, or plants, but also (with the field-bodies of) crystals, minerals, metals, water or other physical objects that appear to be dead from the perspective of normal human consciousness. Clearly, our objective automated weighing research into subtle matter might well provide a key to an extended intellectual and holistic understanding of Nature.

Higher States of Consciousness:
A much more efficient and powerful door opener may be the subjective expansion referred to as higher states of human consciousness. Indications are that in such higher states of consciousness, this infinity of universal subtle life can be cognized directly and experienced without any intellectual effort. Also, telepathic channels to various levels of local or far distant field-bodies can be used for direct intelligent communication.

The monk **Giordano Bruno,** who lived in 16th century Italy, is one historical figure purported to have achieved such a higher state of consciousness. Obviously endowed with extrasensory perception, while looking at the night sky, he declared that the stars were just distant Suns surrounded by their own exoplanets. He raised the possibility that these planets could (and in many cases do) even foster human and other kinds of lifeforms of their own. He also insisted that the Universe is in fact infinite and could have no celestial body at its "center" as was dogmatically declared during his time by the Catholic Church.

Beginning in 1593, Bruno was tried for heresy by the Roman Inquisition on charges including denial of several core Catholic doctrines. Bruno's pantheism was also a matter of grave concern.

The Inquisition found him guilty, and in 1600 he was burned at the stake in Rome's Campo de' Fiori, where today his bronze statue is situated. After his death he gained considerable fame, being particularly celebrated by 19th and 20th Century commentators who regarded him as a martyr for science.

Even now science does not understand and could not explain Bruno's altered state of consciousness and vision which allowed him to cognize the Universe as a living being.

As indicated schematically in Fig. 32, based on the discovery of subtle matter, a solid bridge will be established connecting the visible, materialistic, gross world with the heretofore secret realm of the invisible subjectivity of subtle consciousness.

Based on certain assumptions, modern science has claimed that dark energy and dark matter comprise together about 96 % of the universal mass (please note that this proposed mass and energy are called dark by physics because it is invisible and up to date not detectable by existing astronomical instruments). Our research into subtle matter has given hints that the modern physics proposed and intensively searched for dark energy, seems to be identical with subtle matter with a negative sign (with a contribution of about 73 % of the universal mass). And that the proposed dark matter, seems to be identical with subtle matter with a positive sign (with a contribution of about 23 % of the universal mass), most likely representing forms of life and consciousness. But the field-like quanta of subtle matter with macroscopic mass are, if at all, hard to detect using CERN's technology.

Thus, it becomes imaginable that consciousness, in the form of both dark energy and dark matter, permeates the Universe. Consciousness may not only permeate the Universe, it might also dominate its large scale structures. Our research hints that normal matter, which makes up about 4 % of the Universe's mass, emerges from the properties or effects of subtle matter.

Therefore, we come to the surprising, but experimentally supported conclusion, that the Universe is 100 % dominated by the effects of consciousness, i.e. it is solely based on subtle negentropic and subtle entropic matter.

Near Death Experience (NDE) and Out of Body Experience (OBE):

NDE is a personal experience associated with impending death, encompassing sensations that include detachment from the body or, for example, feelings of levitation or being outside the body, etc. Subjective reports indicate that such experiences often happen in a clinic. People report observing doctors and nurses and hearing what they say, often from a position above the room and outside their physical body.

OBE is a similar experience of usually healthy people that typically involves also a sensation of floating outside one's gross body and, in some cases, perceiving one's physical body from a place above one's body. It seems that in NDE as well as in OBE, consciousness continues despite lack of gross neuronal activity in the brain, as documented for example by the Dutch scientist Pim van Lommel. Such phenomena cannot be explained by modern medicine, even though speculative explanations are given, ranging from fantasy based hallucinations to the release of special neuronal hormones in the brain.

Fig. 34: Explanation of near-death experiences (NDE) and out-of-body experiences (OBE)

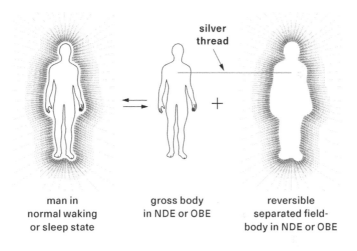

silver thread

| man in normal waking or sleep state | gross body in NDE or OBE | reversible separated field-body in NDE or OBE |

In Fig. 34 a graphic explanation of NDE and OBE is presented. This is based on our experimental results which show the existence of the subtle-matter human field-body. In death the field-body irreversibly separates from the gross physical body.

However, under special circumstances of high stress, as with NDE, or, if the person has highly developed mental sensitivity, as with OBE, this separation from the gross physical body is reversible.

This explains NDE or OBE and allows us to understand why a person undergoing NDE or OBE can see their gross physical surroundings and may hear and understand what is being said by others nearby.

This is because, in such states of consciousness, seeing and hearing can continue to work in the field-body via the non-electromagentic subtle matter processes of the beams of sight and the beams of hearing.

On the other hand, the field-body of a person in NED or OBE, after (reversible) separation from the gross body, is invisible to "normal persons" such as doctors or nurses because it does not reflect electromagnetic radiation in the range of visible light (unless, of course, any of the doctors or nurses might have paranormal abilities to consciously use their beam of sight in the visual process).

The line in the above sketch between the gross body and the field-body indicates the reversibility of the separation between the two bodies, and is often described as a connective (subtle) "silver-thread".

If a person is not fatally ill, he or she has a negentropically dominated field-body. This implies in NDE, for example, that the subtle, invisible field-body, after its separation, experiences an anti-gravitational force in the gravitational field of the Earth, and starts to levitate. The gravitational effect of negentropic subtle matter has already been proven in our experiments by the measured mass changes of different types of detectors.

Of special interest in NDE's are reports of seeing light, and feeling an intelligent "communication with light".

This vision of "light" may in fact result from "rays" of non-electromagnetic subtle matter.

Such reports again give credence to the above hypothesis that "fields of subtle matter are intelligent fields of consciousness", being the non-electromagnetic subtle "light of life". This supports the understanding that fields of subtle matter, especially the negentropic fields, are the essential basis for the existence of life in the Universe, in superposition with gross physical bodies or without such bodies.

Fig. 35: Birth, death and rebirth

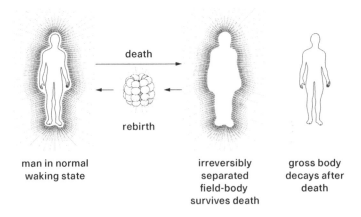

man in normal   irreversibly   gross body
waking state   separated   decays after
                             field-body   death
                             survives death

If the separation of the field-body from the physical body occurs irreversibly, death of a person (or any living being) results. In Fig. 35 this situation is schematically shown.

The gross body decays after death, whilst the field-body survives death. Such a human survival of death is accepted in many societies around the World, from ancient times to the present day.

In modern science there is still no place for such an understanding. According to the mainstream neuroscientific view, once the brain stops functioning at brain death, consciousness fails to survive and ceases to exist. Thus, in mainstream science, human life begins with a fertilized egg and it ends after death, without any further traces of its former existence. This understanding changes with the discovery that the invisible human field-body consists of real mass that can be weighed.

Based on our understanding of the subtle field-body and its stability independent of gross matter, one can begin to verify ancient beliefs. For example, the constantly evolving individual field-body appears not only to exist now, but to be immortal, possibly having existed from ancient times throughout the course of time until today, and will continue to exist in the future.

From time to time the field-body (or soul), existing in invisible dimensions, may associate with a fertilized egg to get a new physical body. All such experiences from former lives and the present life seem to be stored in the field-body. Such reflections are not of a speculative esoteric nature, but follow from the properties of subtle matter and the now proven existence of the subtle field-body.

Another point of interest in this regard is that, according to mainstream science and education the responsibility of individuals for any unethical, aggressive, etc. "negative deeds and behavior" ceases to exist after death.

From the above mentioned view of subtle field-bodies, the situation is different. In this case every human being is still responsible for deeds done in earlier lifetimes. It should again be mentioned that the field-bodies of animals and plants also survive death. These considerations match the belief-system regarding karma, which is still lively in many Eastern cultures.

What we have outlined here are conclusions in accord with our research into subtle matter. Further research described under the following topics and sections is necessary to deepen our understanding of invisible processes at the various levels of subtle matter in connection with physical effects in the gross visible World.

3 Subtle Matter Proof in Purely Physical or Chemical Experiments

So far we have described the surprising discovery of subtle matter in the life of humans, animals and plants and have shown it to have some of the qualities associated with consciousness. One may wonder as to how subtle matter interacts with non-sentient gross matter. In fact this area opens up another wide field of research into the characteristics of subtle matter.

3.1 Results Challenging the Law of Conservation of Mass

Rigourous, Artifact-free Scientific Research:
Our experimental weighing methods are completely within the concepts of modern physics. However, the unexpected and surprising gravitational anomalies shown by our detectors take us out of the current scientific paradigm.

Therefore we now have to consider our results, formulate a consistent theory, and extend the concepts of modern physics.

In the following pages we are going to describe some of our purely physical and chemical experiments and their results. All our weighing experiments were carefully designed to exclude all factors that might cause artifacts. Initially, we conducted a series of different baseline experiments using samples which contained no phase boundaries (see Section 4.3, Phase Boundaries) to exclude any known physical effects that might be responsible for the results. Then an intensive research program was performed to exclude any known physical effects that might be responsible for artifactual influences.

This was necessary to be certain that any anomalous weight changes represented true deviations from the conservation laws of modern physics. It was found that the following known physical effects were not involved in the generation of measured mass deviations:

▷ Electromagnetic effects (tests with discharging batteries in air-tight glass flasks)

▷ Influences of light fields

▷ Static or dynamic temperature effects (all tests were performed under temperature equilibrium)

▷ Variable atmospheric conditions, including buoyancy-effects

▷ Pressure changes within a flask (tests with an internal pressure increase of up to 3 bar showed no effect)

▷ Varying rates of the absorption of water at the external surface of the test flasks (condensation)

▷ Time dependent maximum changes of Earth's acceleration

Fig. 36: Baseline test; mass changes of the detector in the range of ±2 microgram

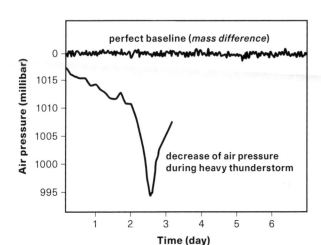

The horizontal measuring curve in Fig. 36 shows results from measuring cycles using the Comparator (weighing accuracy, plus or minus 1 microgram; see 4.2, Weighing Equipment) with four identical empty, air-tight and closed test flasks (50 ml each) that did not contain any phase boundaries other than those between air and glass that were identical for the four flasks.

This entire baseline weighing process lasted about 7 days and was undertaken to check the accuracy of the experimental equipment. Two flasks were weighed as a "reference system" and two flasks served as "test system".

By subtracting the initial mass difference between the test flasks and the reference samples from all following mass differences obtained, a horizontal baseline was obtained, as can be seen in the upper part of the graph.

151

As would be expected, the weight difference between the test and reference samples remained constant, and a straight baseline was obtained over the 7 days.

Even a passing thunderstorm, indicated in the graph by the significant drop of the air pressure, did not influence the weighing baseline. This confirmed that the balance worked properly and was fully protected (by a fully closed balance housing) against outside influences. The resulting straight baseline is in agreement with the expected conservation of mass in closed systems under isothermic conditions, as known from current physics, i.e. from the first law of thermodynamics.

Fig. 37: Unexpected mass increase of the detector

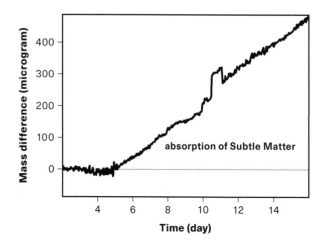

In the next experiment, see Fig. 37, the measuring results of comparing an empty reference flask with an internally silver-plated test flask (the "detector"), both sealed and gas-tight are shown.

The test (as all other tests) was again done under iso-thermal conditions within the protective wooden box in which the scale was firmly mounted to a wall. The internal silver-plating to produce the phase boundaries (see Section 4.3, Phase Boundaries) of the detector flask was applied some hours prior to the baseline testing. This was done by mixing aqueous solutions of glucose and Tollen's reagent in the flask (see Wikipedia for "Tollens' reagent").

This method of "internal silver plating" is a standard procedure in chemistry. The resulting chemical reac-tion produces a thin layer of pure silver on the inside wall of the glass flasks (the treated glass flasks look like Christmas tree balls). This produces the necessary phase boundary, which is the contact area between the internal glass wall and the metallic silver layer.

In general all such areas between layers of two dif-ferent substances work as "phase boundaries". Subtle matter, for as yet unknown reasons, tends to bind readily to certain phase boundaries. After silver-plat-ing, the gas tight test flasks were emptied, and then tightly closed.

The initial mass difference between the detector flask and the reference sample was then subtracted from each of the automatic test measurements in the experiment. Thereby, we could test the theory that subtle matter binds to the silver/glass phase boundary. This was clearly shown by the weight increase of the test flask, when compared with the static weight of the non silver-plated reference flask. A weighing cycle took some minutes and was repeated automatically over a period of about 15 days.

During the first five days, no significant weight change occurred, and a baseline was established (see Fig. 37). This indicates that subtle processes may need some time to start and proceed. But afterwards, the mass of the silver-plated test flask systematically increased to values up to +500 micrograms (µg).

Clearly visible in the results are "step-by-step" mass changes in the time periods between days 4 and 5 as well as around day 11. These are the first signs that subtle matter may be quantized.

The deviations from the baseline give credit to the hypothesis that an invisible matter with easily measurable mass was absorbed by the detector, presumably at the phase boundary of the internal silver-plating.

A great number of additional tests confirmed the hypothesis that subtle matter, in non-living, purely physical systems, can be absorbed at phase boundaries. These additional tests were repeated using a variety of different detectors (see Section 4.4, Detectors for Subtle Matter), different weighing systems, and under different environmental conditions.

Fig. 38 shows measuring results from a more sophisticated test with the Comparator. In this trial, the aqueous Tollen's solution to produce the silver plating inside the test flask was first poured into the flask. The second reagent (the "glucose solution") was kept in a small glass beaker standing in the Tollen's solution at the bottom of the closed gas-tight test flask. Additionally, the test flask contained about 200 mg of finely ground diamond dust to significantly increase the silver plated phase boundary surface area.

Fig. 38: Intense weight fluctuation

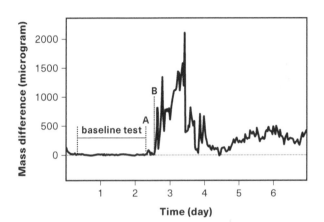

This setup allowed us to establish a baseline before creating the phase boundaries by silver plating the test flask and its diamond dust contents.

The resulting stable pre-test baseline shown in Fig. 38 confirmed the correct functioning of the balance and, as expected, followed the law of conservation of mass, i.e. there was no weight change of the test flask in comparison to the empty reference flask. After about two days of no weight changes, at time A, the test flask was taken out of the Comparator with a pair of tweezers and was slowly turned around, so that the aqueous glucose solution flowed out of the small beaker and was mixed with the Tollen's reagent. Due to this mixing of the chemicals, the reaction started, and both the interior of the still-closed gas-tight glass flask and the diamond dust were silver plated.

After mounting the test flask again on the balance and waiting for some hours for the test flask to reach thermal equilibrium, the test was continued from time B. Almost immediately very significant mass changes were seen, ranging in peak-value up to about $+2000\,\mu g$. This is in sharp contrast to our previously mentioned experiment (see Fig. 37).

These results give credit to the hypothesis that, at newly generated phase boundaries, subtle matter can be absorbed more quickly. Also, the increased phase boundary surface area due to the presence of diamond dust likely contributed to the rapidity and intensity of the observed weight deviations.

Many tests were done also with rolled detectors. These were made of thin metal foil rolled into cylinders of about 3 cm in diameter and about 18 cm long. In this next test, the rolled detector was made from two sheets of PET (Polyethylene terephthalate) alternating with two sheets of aluminium foil, each sheet about 145 cm × 16 cm. They were tightly rolled onto a glass tube, which was afterwards removed. This produced rolled phase boundaries between the sheets of PET and aluminium.

Fig. 39 shows results of a weighing test with such a detector-roll, in comparison to a reference sample made of the same materials, of the same sizes, which was not rolled but folded together. The folded aluminum foil with alternating PET sheets did not produce a comparable structure with geometric phase boundaries. Separate tests of the equipment with a sensitive coulomb meter prior to the weighing test showed that the samples carried no electrostatic charges.

Fig. 39: Measuring effects using a Aluminium-foil detector

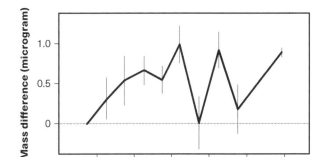

This, and many other identical experiments were conducted over periods of several days. The results all clearly support the hypothesis that subtle matter exhibits a "shape-dependent", i.e. "form-specific" (or "topological") physical interaction with phase boundaries of gross matter, and that it possesses a macroscopically weighable mass. The results clearly show a daily rhythm, which also appeared in a number of other tests performed during the same year.

Fig. 40 shows the results from another automated weighing experiment, using an aluminum roll-detector test sample compared with a folded reference sample as described above. Our question was: do subtle matter fields exchange any kind of subtle field-information with one another without being in direct physical contact?

Fig. 40: Subtle matter fields can influence each other

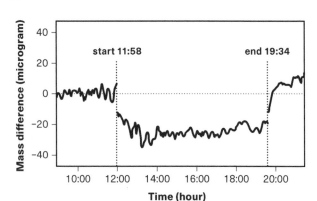

After establishing a stable baseline, a second roll detector identical to the test sample in the balance was carefully positioned side by side, parallel to the test sample. The approaching roll was moved slowly towards the test sample moving from 15 cm away to 5 mm away, over about 5 seconds, always being parallel to one another, and with no mechanical contact between the rolls. At a separation distance of 5 mm, the weight of the test sample roll fell by about 30 microgram. When the second roll-detector was removed after about 8 hours, the test detector's original weight was reached again. Independent control tests had previously shown that such roll-detectors carry no electrostatic charges.

Therefore, it is plausible that the weight deviations occurred due to subtle matter fields. If this is true, this result would indicate the presence of a measurable, macroscopic subtle "field-field" interaction between the two field-bodies bound to each of the rolls. Whenever two field-bodies come close enough we always expect that this kind interaction is happening.

Fig. 41: More about subtle matter fields influencing each other

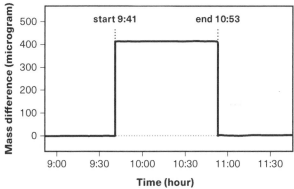

Weighing tests indicate that metals are also carriers of subtle field-bodies that are bound by form-specific interaction with their internal phase boundaries. We found this especially with iron and iron alloys, presumably due to internal phase boundaries between differently oriented crystallized regions, or "Weiss domains".

159

In support of these assertions, Fig. 41 shows mass changes in a weighing test with the two-pan micro balance where a non-magnetizable, circular flat stainless steel plate (17.85 gram, diameter 3.8 cm) was used as a detector. After recording a stable baseline, a massive iron-cylinder (816.31 g, diameter about 4 cm) was co-axially moved from a distance of about 15 cm away to a distance of about 5 mm from the stainless steel plate, without any mechanical contact between the two objects.

At the moment that the separation distance reached 5 mm, a sudden weight jump of +426 microgram occurred. The weight immediately dropped back to the baseline when the iron cylinder was again drawn back. Both, the stainless steel detector and the iron-cylinder were carefully electrically grounded prior to the test so that no electrical charges could influence the result.

Fig. 42: Mass changes of a steel sample when an iron-cylinder was approaching or departing stepwise

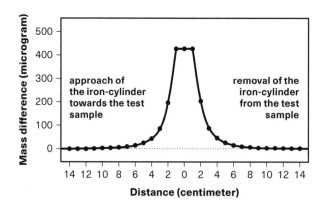

Using the same apparatus as that used for the Fig. 41 test, with the separation distance between the cylinder and the plate being changed by 1 cm steps, the results shown in Fig. 42 were produced. The results indicate that the field of subtle matter bound to the iron sample must have a macroscopic spatial extension in a range of 10 cm or more.

Fig. 43: Subtle matter forms quanta

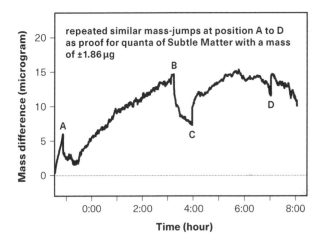

Fig. 43 shows the results of a weighing experiment using liquid crystals in solid form as the test detector. Liquid crystals are well known as LCD, i.e. liquid crystal displays. They can, despite the name "liquid" also exist in solid form at normal temperatures. The perfectly ordered geometrical structure of such crystals produces excellent phase boundaries for use in weighing experiments. Again, a wide range of possible research fields may open using this kind of detector.

At times A, B, C, and D in this figure weight-jumps with recurring values were recorded. This pattern also recurred over a number of tests. In further tests with liquid crystals and internally silverplated glas flasks, different sets of mass changes in steps were recorded, however each with a different jump size.

In total, at least three sets of quantized subtle matter mass jump values have been discovered so far. These and many of our other results indicate that subtle matter is quantized. By determining the values of the quanta found in many weighing experiments, we could specify three distinct sizes: $\pm 21.5\,\mu g$, $\pm 1.87\,\mu g$ and $\pm 0.36\,\mu g$.

Besides the detected three "field-quanta" (or "space-quanta") of subtle matter, there are theoretical indications that more such quanta may exist, with mass contents of $< 0.1\,\mu g$ or up to 1 gram. See Table 1 in Section 5.1 of the Appendix for an interesting correlation that was found between the experimentally measured and the theoretically described values of various subtle field-quanta!

Our results show that subtle quanta can have a positive or negative sign with respect to their gravitational effect, yielding therefore gravitational (with positive sign = weight increasing) or anti-gravitational, i.e. repulsive (with negative sign = weight reducing) effects with respect to gross matter. Field-quanta with negative sign may also associate among each other by gravitational force, or possibly by other interactions.

As already mentioned, additional tests reveal that such field-quanta can form associations similar to the way atoms can associate to form molecules, and that such clusters can re-arrange to form new structures.

This evidence for quantization of the subtle matter fields of both types (i.e. those carrying the plus sign and those carrying the negative sign) may give further credence to the proposal that these types of matter are candidates for the so called dark matter and dark energy proposed by cosmologists.

Certain astrophysical observations have been interpreted as support for the existence of both dark matter and dark energy, yet a bench scale proof of existence of dark matter and dark energy, as well as an approach to their description, has been missing.

Quantization is also a property of ordinary matter fields. Within the framework of the so-called Standard Model of Elementary Particles, quantization also is expected in the case of dark matter and dark energy. Thus, these bench scale studies indicating quantization of the two forms of subtle matter may be directly relevant to the quest for dark matter and dark energy.

The search for dark matter and energy is currently based on the assumption that they can be detected as point-like particles within the framework of the Standard Model of Elementary Particles. This research is most notably carried on at CERN, and in other high energy laboratories.

3.2 Solar and Lunar Eclipses: Mysterious Weight Changes

We have already discussed the influence of constellations and the positions of the Moon and Sun on plants and other living beings. Based on interesting historic discoveries, our experiments have shown that the binding of subtle matter to a plant can directly be proven by high precision weighing experiments.

Thus, in principle, weighing experiments can be used to study the effects of constellations and the positions of the Sun and Moon.

Fig. 44: One month weighing experiment showing significant weight increase

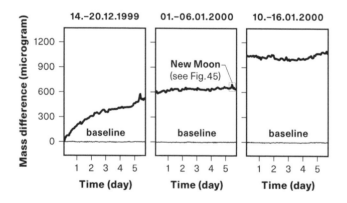

Results of another two-pan balance experiment that was conducted over one month can be seen in Fig. 44. Initially a perfect baseline was established (the lower

line at the bottom of each chart) using two, closed, gas-tight empty glass flasks.

The graphs also show the weighing results, over a period of about four weeks, with an internally silver-plated glass flask as the test sample and a second identical flask as the reference sample which was filled with water to reach the same weight as the test sample.

In this case, the mass of the test flask increased over time, from its initial value up to the plateau values of about +1100 micrograms. This implies a very significant violation of the law of conservation of mass. In our view, this indicates the continuous absorption of an invisible "factor", i.e. invisible subtle matter with macroscopic mass, at the silver metallic phase boundaries.

Fig. 45: Weighing effect during a new moon period (enhanced detail of Fig. 44)

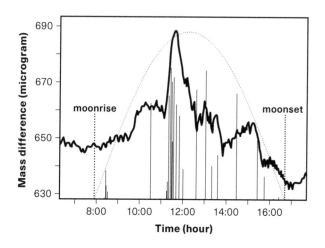

Besides that, a very interesting detail was observed in the test cycle during the third week in a new moon phase. The enlargement of the peak during this new moon phase is shown in Fig. 45. A significant change in the test sample weight curve was observed.

The dotted, sine curve in Fig. 45 indicates the height of the Moon during its passage from moon-rise to moon-set. The weighing curve of the test sample shows a significant mass variation during this period. The overall mass changes not only correlate with the rising and setting of the new moon, but they also correlate with the lunar occlusion of galactic background stars. Their temporal positions are indicated in the graph by solid vertical lines.

The Fig. 45 test results give strong support to the following interpretations: a) that not only was there a positive subtle matter field effect of lunar origin influencing the silver-plated test sample, but also, b) the subtle radiation of galactic background stars produced several small but sharp peak-mass-increases and especially a strong increase of the test sample shortly before 12 o'clock.

The correlation between the observed lunar peaks and of the covering of galactic background stars is a first indication that all galactic stars, like our Sun, are seemingly emitting a subtle matter radiation that exists in addition to that of our own Sun and Moon.

This leads us to propose the existence of a previously unknown to science, all pervading, invisible, yet real, universal subtle background radiation with a positive sign. These observations may even support a mechanism for gravity known as the "Le-Sage-mechanism" (see Wikipedia for "Le Sage's theory of gravitation").

This theory proposed a mechanical explanation for Newton's gravitational force in terms of (previously speculatively assumed, but now experimentally detected) streams of tiny unseen particles. In 1768, Le Sage called his particles "ultra-mundane corpuscles", which impact all material objects from all directions.

According to this model, any two material bodies partially shield each other from the impinging corpuscles, resulting in a net imbalance in the pressure exerted by the impact of corpuscles on the bodies, tending to drive the bodies together. A mathematical analysis of Le Sage's mechanism corresponds exactly with Newton's law of gravity.

The results of physical experiments are not usually dependent on the position of celestial bodies in the solar system. An exception is the well-known case of the lunar tidal forces in the oceans.

However, in the Fig. 47 experiment, for the first time, our results indicate that subtle matter radiation is a phenomenon that includes effects from celestial bodies at the galactic scale. These entropic effects appear to be produced by a predominance of subtle radiation of the weight increasing, positive sign, which is emitted by all celestial bodies.

Due to the gravitational interaction of subtle matter with gross matter, it can be inferred that subtle matter, bound to the center of mass of the Sun, and indeed, to all celestial bodies, is generating large field-bodies around these objects and therefore making them living beings, of a sort.

Subtle matter is expected to be bound similarly not only to stars but also to neutron stars, brown dwarfs, etc., even to galaxies and the postulated black holes.

Our observations thus far, lead us to propose the following: Subtle matter is more strongly attracted to gravitational fields than it is to geometrical form-specific shapes. Therefore, on average, we would expect that the positive sign, entropic, subtle matter field-bodies of stars would be more intense than their negentropic counterparts.

Our research has shown that gross matter, exposed to mechanical shock, will, to some extent, emit subtle matter that was previously bound to it. Our Sun and all stars are continuously exposed to internal shock waves due to turbulent thermal processes. They will therefore constantly emit subtle matter with positive sign (entropic).

This radially emitted universal subtle radiation could be experimentally found in all tests conducted during solar eclipses. Nevertheless, most of the galactic stars, such as the Sun, may certainly possess also sub-dominant, negentropic field-bodies. But these having on average lower subtle field-intensities than their entropic counterparts with a positive sign.

So, in principle, both types of subtle matter are radially emitted into the Sun's surroundings along with the known emissions of electromagnetic radiation and charged particles (solar wind).

Direct detection of solar subtle matter radiation should be possible when the Sun is partially or totally eclipsed by the Moon, as well as during solar transits of Mercury or Venus, for example, or in biological tests, cf. Fig. 25.

Visible total solar eclipses present a great opportunity for such subtle matter measurements because the center of mass of the Sun, the Moon and, with some planning, an observer on Earth can be directly in line with each other, as indicated in Fig. 46.

Fig. 46: Gravitational focussing of solar subtle matter radiation with a positive sign during a solar eclipse, and gravitational scattering of solar non-electromagnetic subtle matter radiation with a negative sign

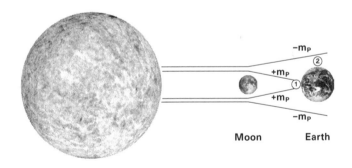

The positive (entropic, weight increasing) type of solar subtle matter radiation (shown in the above illustration as "$+m_P$") and the negative (negentropic, weight reducing) type of subtle matter (shown as "$-m_P$") reach the Moon from the Sun in parallel rays.

In this case, the Moon gravitationally produces a focusing diffraction of the solar subtle matter radiation with a positive sign.

This yields a gravitational increase in the intensity of the subtle $+m_P$-matter radiation with a positive sign at the site of observation for observers at position No. 1.

As subtle matter with positive (= weight increasing) sign exhibits entropic, life weakening influences, this gives us a new understanding as to why, historically, solar eclipses are believed to have a negative influence on human health, especially when looking directly towards the Sun (even with a darkened glass protection).

On the other hand, the Moon gravitationally generates a scattering dissipation of the solar subtle $-m_P$-matter radiation with negative sign. Thus, for an observer at position No. 2 an increased intensity of subtle matter with negative sign will be observed. This increase of negentropic subtle matter, has a life supporting and healing influence.

It should be clarified, that both types of solar subtle matter radiation, traveling in parallel rays, are not bent by the Moon's gross matter, but by its own field of subtle matter.

Similarly, any earthbound observer will be exposed to these diffractive and dissipative effects of the universal subtle matter background radiation with respect to all the celestial bodies in the solar system (the Sun and the Moon included, and ranging from Mercury through Pluto).

Since our first discovery of the Moon's influence on weighing test results, we have performed many tests during visible Solar eclipses, and have amassed a great amount new information regarding the properties of subtle matter fields with respect to celestial bodies in our solar system.

Fig. 47: Weighing test during a total solar eclipse

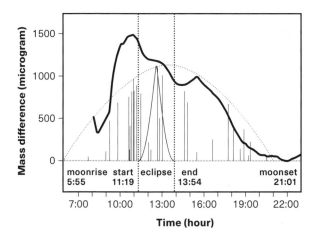

Fig. 47 shows results from a weighing test with the two-pan balance and an internally silver-plated flask as a detector, made during the visible solar eclipse of Aug. 11, 1999 in Germany, at a position equivalent to position No. 1 as shown in Fig. 46. The occlusion of the Sun at the test site measured 99.9 %.

During the maximum coverage of the eclipse, at about half past 12 o'clock a weight change at the detector of about +1200 microgram was recorded. We interpreted this again to mean that the Sun is an emitter of subtle matter, which produces a reversible weight increase, by transferring a real positive momentum to the detector.

Also, a maximum mass increase at the detector of up to about +1500 microgram was observed at about 11:00 h, prior to the maximum of the solar eclipse, at circa 13:30 h (see the dotted curve in Fig. 47). Subsequent study of the astronomical data for that day clearly showed that the maximum weight change of about +1500 µg, between 10:30 and 11:30, correlates with an accumulation of galactic background stars also being occluded by the Moon at that time. The intensity of this covering of background stars is again shown in the graph by the solid vertical lines.

This shows again that not only does the Sun emit a form of subtle matter radiation, but also do all distant stars. From the point of view of present-day physics, however, the observed weight changes clearly violate the law of conservation of momentum.

Fig. 48 shows the results of another test with the same scale and detector as in Fig. 47 made during a visible Solar eclipse in Germany, October 1996. Again, this test revealed that not only did the Moon covering the Sun influence the mass of our test sample, but also the Moon occluding distant stars. It can be seen that, from the start of the eclipse after the time around 15:15, a steady increase in the weight of the test sample occurred. The peak of the weight increase correlates nearly exactly with the degree of maximum solar coverage at 16:31.

Fig. 48: Another weighing test during a partial Solar eclipse

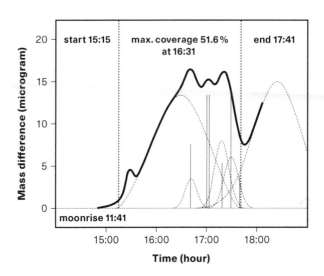

As in the previous experiments, a coverage of background stars also occurred, again producing a "fingerprint" of additional weight peaks at the test sample. The periods of time where the Moon covered the galactic background stars are again indicated by the thin lines of the wave like curves in our graph. Each peak of these thin curves indicates the maximum covering of a specific galactic star by the Moon.

It is of special interest, that for the first small peak of the mass change curve (at about 15:20), no corresponding known background star that could have generated this peak seems to exist.

We can raise the question as to whether we have detected a so far unknown celestial object that could not be detected by its light emission in astrophysical telescopes or if there is some other explanation.

From the results depicted in this experiment, it is again concluded that not only do our Moon and Sun possess one or more subtle field-bodies, but also so do galactic celestial bodies that are many light years away from us. The evidence for this is provided by the documented correlation of the weight peaks with the star occlusions.

The question might occur as to why in this test the maximum weight difference peaked at about 15 µg, while in Fig. 47 a maximum of 1500 µg was measured. The difference between these two eclipses was that the one shown in Fig. 47 was nearly 100 % in its coverage, but the one shown in Fig. 48 was only 51.6 % coverage.

Thus, it is understandable from Fig. 46 that the perfect focusing of the Sun's subtle matter radiation during the complete covering by the Moon in Fig. 47 could explain the difference in recorded peak heights. In Fig. 49 the results of another test made during the solar eclipse of Jan. 4, 2011 are presented. The test was done with the two-pan balance under similar conditions to those described above, using a roll-detector as test sample.

The interesting feature of this test was that the eclipse started 30 minutes before sunrise. Maximum coverage was reached 55 minutes after sunrise, corresponding to the position No. 2 as marked in Fig. 46. In this case no clear "fingerprint" from the occlusion of galactic background stars can be seen in the weighing results.

Fig. 49: Weight decreased when the eclipse started prior to sunrise

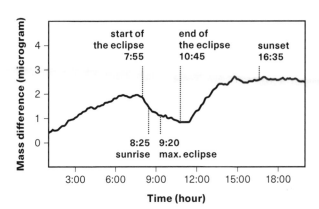

To explain the differences in the results of the last three experiments, it is helpful to study Fig. 46 again. The positive Subtle Matter radiation from the Sun and background galactic stars is focused by the Moon's subtle matter field to an inline observer on the Earth (see the position No. 1), while the negative solar radiation is scattered away to the outside (i.e. to position No. 2).

However, during the experiment shown in Fig. 49, the position of the global observer was in an area which is indicated in Fig. 46 as "No. 2". At these points of observation, an accumulation of the solar subtle matter radiation with a negative sign (weight reducing) occurred during the eclipse, yielding a reversible reduction in the detector's mass during the eclipse.

This unusual, somewhat counter-intuitive process may be difficult to grasp at first. It seems that a transfer of negative momentum occurred in which the detector

175

was not pushed away from the incoming negentropic subtle matter stream, becoming heavier, but being attracted, i.e. becoming lighter.

Such a transfer of negative momentum is completely unknown in modern physics. Yet, the considerations derived from Fig. 46 give a plausible physical interpretation of the different effects observed in the three experiments, and experimentally confirm the existence of a negative, yet weighable, subtle transfer of momentum.

The observed results of Fig. 49 reveal that a Solar subtle negentropic radiation (weight reducing i.e. with a negative sign) exists besides the stronger Solar radiations with a positive sign and weight increasing, as deduced form the results in Fig. 47 and 48. This proof of existence is consistent with the data shown in Fig. 25.

Similar measuring effects as displayed in Fig. 47 and 48 (with a transfer of a positive subtle momentum) could be observed during solar transits of Mercury and Venus. But again, as in the cases described above, further research into eclipse and other transit-processes will open a wide range of new discoveries in subtle matter, especially when such studies are simultaneously performed at various locations on Earth.

In Fig. 50, test-results of another test during the visible, partial Solar eclipse of March 20, 2015 are depicted. In this test an internally silver-plated glass ampule detector was used. This detector had previously been used for several years in many of our weighing experiments. Near the maximum lunar coverage of the

Sun, around time c, again, a significant negative mass change occurred.

However, similar mass changes also can be seen at three other times, cf. times d, e, and f. They may be due to lunar occlusion of galactic background stars. But in comparison to our previous results, some major differences are clear.

Fig. 50: A special subtle effect of the silver-plated detector

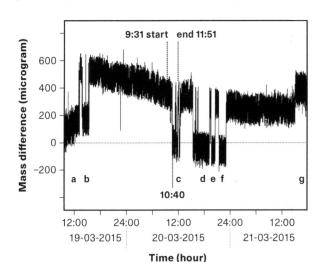

First, the mass of the test sphere fluctuated continuously throughout the experiment. This may have resulted from the assimilation of both plus and minus subtle matter quanta over the 19-year storage period. Similar mass fluctuations of subtle matter were observed in other tests as a result of the superposition of at least two fields of subtle matter in mutual interactions with each other.

Second, the mass reduction at position c, of about 350 µg, does not occur in a smooth process, but in a kind of a stepwise, quantized jump. This may be because the long term "resident" subtle matter quanta generate a resistance to the absorption of further field-quanta, until the intensity of the new incoming subtle matter field reaches a certain threshold. In newly fabricated detectors, as used in the tests of Fig. 47 and 48, such an effect could therefore not occur, and has not yet been observed.

Third, at the center of the Sun's eclipse (at 10:40 on 20-03-2015), a negative mass deviation took place, and not a positive one. This may result from the selection of previously absorbed field-quanta. However, this hypothesis needs further experimental tests before a conclusion can be reached.

3.3   Other Surprising Behavior of Subtle Matter

Soon during the course of our experiments it became obvious that subtle matter does not always just increase the weight of a detector during a test. We observed that the weight might decrease, but later increase again. Besides that, the weight could fluctuate for a while, showing up- or down-jumps; it could also stabilize, after absorption of subtle matter, at a certain plateau level – and so on.

The weight could also decrease for a long period, the limit of which remains unknown, of up to several hundred grams, even in the range of kilograms, as seen in the weighing tests with meditating persons.

All the above are violations of the law of conservation of mass. Our findings clearly show that there is a lot more to be studied to gain a complete understanding of subtle matter. These studies could include for example more research on the influence of constellations of planets and stars, and might thereby lead to a new understanding of astrology.

With regard to the weight reduction due to the absorption of subtle matter, we suggest that the reader familiarize him or herself with the summary of subtle matter properties as so far discovered (see Section 5.4).

The weight-reducing influence of subtle matter is entropy-reducing (herein called "negentropic"). Negentropic subtle matter produces growth, regeneration, healing and life-supporting influences in biological systems. For these reasons our research thus far has been focused on the effects of negentropic subtle matter, as opposed to entropic subtle matter.

Fig. 51 depicts a short period from another automatic weighing experiment with the two-pan balance that ran for several weeks. During this time, again and again bursts of intense mass fluctuations, of the type seen above, were repeatedly recorded. The detector in this experiment was a saturated aqueous solution of sodium chloride (salt, NaCl) in a gas-tight glas ampoule.

Fig. 51: Results with fluctuating mass changes

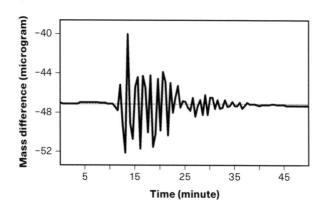

Obviously, the phase boundary between the water molecules and the dissolved salt crystals (and their clustering in the aqueous solution, yielding also strong phase boundaries) improves the ability of pure water to bind subtle matter. Again, the test sample, in a closed gastight glass-ampule, was compared with a volume-identical, closed gas-tight, but empty glass-ampule. The weight difference was measured and recorded automatically every 30 seconds.

The origin of these recorded bursts of "subtle matter radiation" is at present unknown.

To localize the source of these bursts it would be helpful to install a network of similar balances at various distances from each other (even on different continents) to simultaneously perform a sequence of similar measurements at the same time. This could help to clarify the question as to whether the origin of the bursts is due to a local, global or cosmic signal.

We feel that this approach could lead to a very interesting research program, possibly in connection with gravitational waves. Organic compounds can also facilitate the absorption of subtle matter, especially if they create phase boundaries in the form of thin films or micelles. A wide field of research may open in the area of water emulsions. To our knowledge, no such experiments have yet been performed.

Fig. 52: More surprising weighing results

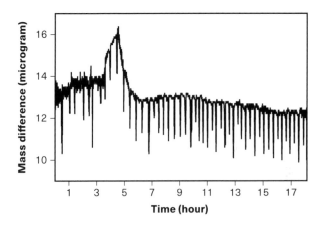

Fig. 52 shows the result of another test with the two-pan balance and a liquid crystal test sample (in solid form) suspended to the balance in a gas-tight aluminium container. A second liquid crystal sample was brought nearby the test sample without mechanical contact. As can be seen, the weight of the test sample continuously exhibited very regular and significant mass oscilliations over many hours.

We feel that the regularity of the oscillations indicates the interaction of two subtle-matter fields of the crystals. It is not yet clear under which conditions this oscillatory interaction between two or more subtle matter fields occurs. Quite possibly, similar oscillations may occur in the organic tissues of living beings, producing for example the so called biological clocks.

4   Summary

In present-day physics, because of their usually low intensity, subtle matter effects either "vanish" in the measuring noise of the gross physical apparatus or they lead to inexplicable, anomalous results that one hopes can be explained later.

On the other hand, our well-established weighing methodologies using high precision balances and special detectors have provided a previously unknown method to facilitate research in this area. The interpretation of weighing anomalies in terms of subtle matter is now backed by many experiments showing predicted results.

The following is an overview of the main properties of subtle matter as detected to date.

#1   Quantized subtle matter with a macroscopically extended field-like structure and macroscopic mass co-exists as a second category of matter besides the ordinary gross matter.

#2   Gross matter always has a positive mass while subtle matter can exhibit either positive or negative mass.
a) Subtle matter with negative mass acts in a weight-reducing and supportive-regenerative, i.e. "negentropic" way on gross matter, including biological systems.

Subtle matter of this type has a positive influence on orderliness and harmonic growth in living systems, enhances health, and exhibits healing qualities. "Negentropy" as used in this book is a quality that reduces disorder (entropy) by increasing the orderliness of a system.

Our shorthand for negentropic subtle matter is: "$-m_P$ **subtle matter**", but the minus-sign comes from its weight-reducing property and does not refer to negative energy or negative charge.

b) Subtle matter with positive mass (i.e. "$+m_P$-**matter**") acts in a weight-increasing way on gross matter or in biological systems. The plus sign comes from the weight-increasing quality.

This form of subtle matter has no "positive" influence on life, instead acting destructively, i.e. "entropically".

#3 Subtle matter can be absorbed at phase boundaries of material surfaces by a form-specific (i.e. topological) interaction (especially if the phase boundary has a geometrical form) or by gravitational interaction (i.e. at celestial bodies) and thereby influences the quality of these objects.

#4 Every object in the Universe, whether we generally call it "living" or "inanimate" carries an invisible subtle-matter field, the "field body" or "pilot field". If the being is in a state of good health, the field is negentropically dominated. This also holds for all subsystems of a body.

It is interesting to note that increased intensity of the weight-increasing positive subtle matter weakens capillary forces in organic and inorganic materials, while that of "negentropic subtle matter" increases the strength of capillary forces.

#5 **Human Consciousness:** Human consciousness is either identical with the subtle field-body of the person or it is interwoven with internal structures of subtle matter of the field-body. The existence of distance healing and telekenetic abilities support this assumption.

#6 Results of **"complementary medicine"** (including alternative medicine and other designations) can be scientifically explained by the detection of the human field-body and other field-bodies in the surroundings which may interact with it.

#7 Right-turning water vortices, according to Viktor Schauberger, can load water with negentropic subtle matter and therefore seems to have positive health effects.

#8 The different field-bodies of the participants of a group or society superimpose to generate a "collective field-body" or "group field of consciousness". So, for example, a family, community, company or nation will each have its own collective field-body. Also communities of animals or plants can be expected to exhibit collective field-bodies (as well as inanimate systems).

#9 The **subtle matter-field** of the Earth may relate to Sheldrake's global morphic field and probably also to the effects of Nelson's Global Consciousness Project (GCP).

#10 The field-bodies of every celestial object in the solar system (and beyond), interact with each other and with every object on Earth. This holds also for plants, animals, and the human field-bodies as well, and can be seen by the measurable influence of **Solar and Lunar eclipses.**

#11 Any gross matter seems to carry an amount of subtle matter having a weighable mass that can be big or small, positive or negative. These findings of subtle matter effects necessitate an extension of the **laws of thermodynamics,** Newton's **law of gravitation,** and a higher-dimensional extension of **Special Relativity Theory** (see Appendix and our upcoming book on science and subtle matter).

#12 The **three types of field-quanta** we have detected exhibit macroscopic mass and energy and can associate into clusters in the same way as atoms can form molecules. We propose that one such cosmic cluster results in the formation of a highly ordered universal subtle **"ether"** that may supersede the presently assumed universal "vacuum state".

#13 All forms of gross matter emerge from a cosmic **"relativistic ether"** as already predicted and searched for by Albert Einstein. All classical, quantum mechanical or relativistic properties of gross matter emerge from interactive effects of the subtle matter.

#14 The real energy content of subtle matter quanta can be used to generate **free energy**.

#15 High subtle field intensities may allow spontaneous low energy nuclear transmutations (LENR) or anti-gravitative effects.

For a deeper look at the details of our experiments and also at the quantum mechanical analysis of subtle matter, we recommend:

▷ The **Appendix of this book**;

▷ The more scientific documentation provided in the book **"Discovery of Subtle Matter – A short introduction"**, ISBN 978-3-946533-01-6, ASIN B06Y276M81;

▷ The **next book by Dr. Volkamer** which will cover all experiments and the detailed information for scientific readers, planned for release in 2021.

See also more books by Dr. Volkamer, and read excerpts from them, on:

www.brosowski-publishing.com.

4.1 Further Research

We offer our extensive research results to the scientific community and ask that fellow subtle-matter investigators both replicate our results and develop further research programs. This would likely prove to be a highly worthwhile step for modern physics.

So far, the following methods to detect and study subtle matter have been found:

Method #1: Bench scale tests, performing weighing experiments with various gross detectors having geometrically-shaped phase boundaries.

Method #2: Bench scale weighing tests during Solar and Lunar eclipses, or Solar Venus and Mercury transits, etc., or by measuring various physical or physico-chemical parameters during such events.

We propose for example to design a series of simultaneous worldwide weighing tests, performed at carefully chosen locations, during eclipse configurations so that both types of subtle matter can be observed and studied. Section 4.4 gives in the table "Detectable effects of subtle matter" a list of parameters that may be useful in detecting subtle radiation during such eclipses or transits).

Method #3: Bench scale biological weighing experiments with human beings during psychological or parapsychological procedures, or sprouting tests with plant seeds to detect negentropic or entropic effects, either throughout the year or during eclipses, eventually simultaneously at different places on Earth.

Method #4: Testing the effects of negentropically activated water generated from a properly run, right-turning water vortex.

Method #5: Performance of tests by applying Brown's Gas.

In this first book for a general readership, it was possible to give only a basic and easy to understand overview of our research.

4.2 Weighing Equipment

This newly discovered form of matter can be detected by weighing experiments using specific detectors. To weigh subtle matter we used high-precision, modern, laboratory scales for smaller vessels, and for larger bodies we used weighing equipment to sit on or to sleep on.

A) Weighing experiments with persons as detectors:
To measure weight effects of subtle matter on human beings we applied:

1) A "**Chair-Balance**" to weigh persons during meditation and directed thought experiments. A comfortable chair was prepared and mounted on an electronic balance accurate to plus or minus 0.1 gram and was connected to a computer with automatic data recording. The weight was measured frequently, usually every second. A special software program was used to graphically

present the data. Before starting the experimental tests, a baseline was always run to ensure that the equipment worked accurately.

2) A **"Bed-Balance"** for sleep research. Four electronic balances, each accurate to 0.1 gram, were placed under the four feet of the bed. Readings from the four balances were automatically summed, and the totals (with an accuracy of plus or minus 0.2 gram) were stored in sequence by a computer. Again, a special software program was used to graphically present the data.

B) Weighing experiments in the microgram range:
Generally, several types of automatic high-precision laboratory weighing systems with computer data storage were used. These balances were accurate to plus or minus 1 to 2 micrograms (µg). One "microgram" equals one-millionth of a gram, whereas one milligram (mg) equals one thousandth of a gram.

One system used was a **"two-pan balance"** from Sartorius AG, Germany, see Fig. 53a. In this system, one side weighed the detector while the comparison reference was on the other side. Both reference and test samples were suspended from the pans by stainless steel wires. The balance was mounted, via a metal frame, to a firm wall and was placed within a wooden box with a front-door for protection against external influences. Data recording in the range of seconds was automatic, with data storage on a PC.

Fig. 53: a) Two pan balance, and b) Comparator used for the weighing tests, see also Fig. 54

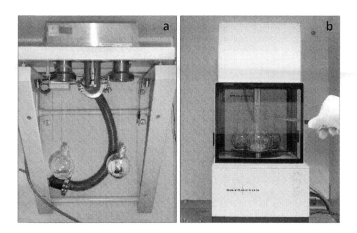

The other type of balance is called a **"comparator"** and works differently; it can weigh 4 samples on a weighing dish. Four samples could be placed on a circular metallic weighing dish. This dish lifted, turned and lowered the four samples by an electronically controlled mechanical gear so that they could be placed sequentially on the weighing pin to be weighed. In this equipment two of the samples were used as reference samples and the other two as detectors. The data were recorded and processed with our software.

As with the former balance, the mass comparator was placed on a metal frame mounted to a firm wall and was protected against external influences by a wooden box with a front door, in addition to the protective housing of the mass comparator itself. Four 50 ml gas-tight glass flasks were usually used in these tests.

One flask, containing inert material such as glass balls, for example, served as the reference system, while in the other flasks newly generated phase boundaries (for example, generated by internal silver plating) served as the detectors for the absorption of subtle matter.

All tests were done under isothermal conditions. In addition to the respective weight of a sample, the date and time of the weighing as well as the temperature, air pressure and humidity inside the wooden weighing box were recorded at each time point.

The data-analysis itself was usually done in the following scientific manner. The weight of the reference sample and the test sample (the "detector") were recorded and one was subtracted from the other at each time point. The subtracted mass difference was drawn, via special software, as a continuous line over the course of the experiment. Normally the mass difference baseline is expected to be straight due to the "law of conversation of mass".

In every test, initially four identical reference samples were used for proving the baseline. This confirmed the accurate working of the apparatus and the correct isolation of the test system from external or artifactual influences.

Some tests were done with a Sartorius (type RC 210S) **one-pan semi-micro balance** with a reproducibility of $\pm 10\,\mu g$ and automated data registration. Also, for some tests, a Mettler (type P 1000) **one-pan mechanical** non-automatic balance with an accuracy of ± 0.1 gram was used. In these cases, for example, test and reference samples were alternately weighed twice daily.

Fig. 54: (a) Sketch of the Comparator, (b) a standing glass flask, and (c) vertical view of the circular platform on which the glass flasks where placed

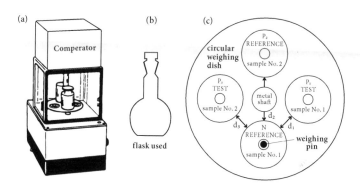

4.3 Phase Boundaries

A "phase boundary," as often mentioned in this book, is the place were two surfaces are in contact but not inter-mixed, such as, for example, when two hands are held together. Subtle matter can be absorbed at all places where two surfaces are in close contact with each other. The contact area, or so to say, the microscopic "gap" between two phases, is the area were subtle matter asso-ciates (or "binds") to gross matter. Phase boundaries exist, for example, in the following contact areas:

▷ from solid to solid

▷ from solid to liquid

▷ from solid to gas

▷ from liquid to gas

▷ from liquid to liquid

▷ within solid crystals such as metals and minerals

▷ within liquid water, where solid water clusters (essentially, very small ice crystals) exist.

Newly created phase boundaries are ideally suited for weighing experiments in the microgram range for detecting the absorption of subtle matter. Reference systems must be without such newly created boundaries.

One quite effective system used in our tests is a gastight closed glass bulb that is newly covered on the inside by chemically generated silver plating, creating an appearance similar to a Christmas tree ball. In this case the newly created phase boundaries are between the silver film and the glass wall and between the silver film and the gas content. These two boundaries are the areas within the bulb to which subtle matter will bind.

The weighing of test systems with newly created phase boundaries in comparison to reference systems without such boundaries allows for the detection of invisible subtle matter in the microgram range. However, as we have already seen, subtle matter may also generate mass effects in the macroscopic range, up to plus or minus 0.5 or 1 kg, and more. From the point of view of physics since early in the 20th century, such measured mass effects violate the law of conservation of mass.

4.4 Detectors for Subtle Matter

As we have seen so far, the weighing tests always need to compare at least two different types of sample object. One being the detector, carrying phase boundaries, the other being the reference sample, without (or with fewer) phase boundaries. Subtle matter will not readily bind via its form-specific interaction unless phase boundaries or electric plasma (for example, in the Sun) are present, and it is more likely to bind if those boundaries are newly created. The following systems (or combinations between them) can be used for the detection of subtle matter:

Chemical systems using gas-tight sealed spherical glass flasks that are freshly silver-plated internally. Other examples include flasks containing freshly silver-plated glass spheres or ground solid materials, when compared with similar glass flasks without any silver-plating. Besides silver, other metals can be applied, for example, gold, copper, etc. Freshly generated crystal precipitations may also work, as do liquid crystals in solid or dissolved form. Additionally, emulsions also work, for example, water in oil or oil in water, especially if such systems are stabilized by emulsifying agents. Subtle matter absorption may be significantly increased by swirling such detector systems.

Physico-chemical detectors, such as, sodium chloride (NaCl), dissolved in water (with variable concentrations, up to saturation) works well as a detector in gas-tight glass flasks or ampoules. Other similar polar compounds that can be dissolved in water may be used as well. Even pure water absorbs subtle matter well, especially after it has been "enlivened" using water-vortices.

Physical systems, such as one or two layers of aluminum foil (such as $16 \times 145\,cm$) separated by polyethylene sheets and rolled together in the shape of a cylinder with about 3 or $8\,cm$ diameter, forming a cylindrical "**roll-detector**"), can be used after grounding and checking with a Coulomb-meter that they do not carry electrostatic charges. For a reference system, similar materials with the same dimensions can be used in a different geometrical shape, i.e. the layers can be folded so that there is only a difference in the shape between the test and reference system. Besides aluminum, other thin metal foils such as gold, silver, copper, etc. all work well. Our tests revealed that the rate of absorption of subtle matter by normal gross matter depends significantly on the geometry of the gross matter used.

The more symmetrical a gross detector is, the higher is the rate of absorption of subtle matter. It is astonishing that such a simple detector can interact with the human field-body!

Biological systems function well as detectors of subtle matter due to internal phase boundaries in the organic structure, i.e. in the cell membranes and cell organelles. Cress seeds, with some droplets of distilled water, can be used in thermodynamically closed systems such as sealed glass ampules, in comparison to similar containers without seeds. Other types of seeds such as mung beans, for example, can work as detectors, and certainly a great variety of other plant seeds may also serve as detectors.

Other plants, and also the human body itself, can work as subtle matter detectors. For humans, one can detect subtle matter by weighing the whole body or by weighing just a drop of dried blood in a sealed ampule.

Measurable Effects of Subtle Matter:
Here follows a further survey about measurable effects under the influence of subtle matter fields which can occur, for example, during solar and lunar eclipses or may be induced under laboratory conditions. Following this we give a brief list of predictions that result from the theory of subtle matter.

The following list is a slightly modified version of a list that was presented, along with our results shown in Fig. 31, for the first time during the Wetsus Water Congress Sept. 2015 in Leeuwarden, Netherlands. The Wetsus institute (see www.wetsus.nl) is described as a european centre of excellence for sustainable water technology. In 2017 the list was published in the book *"Discovery of Subtle Matter, a Short Introduction"*, ISBN 978-3-946533-01-6 (published with kind support of Wetsus).

It should be noted that recently, Westus researchers were able to confirm one point on our list (changes in surface tension) during four solar eclipse events. The results were published in 2019 under the title *"Solar Eclipses and the Surface Properties of Water"*, E. C. Fuchs, et al., in the scientific journal *Earth, Moon, and Planets* –

An International Journal of Solar System Science; see: https://doi.org/10.1007/s11038-019-09529-0. The paper gives various explanation models for the anomaly as found.

Detectable effects of subtle matter	symbol
violations of the law of conservation of mass, i.e. mass changes:	
• form-specific and gravitational interactions of subtle matter	Δm
• field-bodies of gross macroscopic and cosmic systems	Δm
• field-bodies and quantum mechanical entanglement	Δm
• violations of the law of conservation of momentum	$\Delta(m \cdot v)$
violations of the law of conservation of angular momentum	ΔL
changes of temperature due to subtle matter fields	$\Delta T < 0, \ \Delta T > 0$
changes of pH in aqueous solutions due to subtle matter fields	ΔpH
changes of the redox potential in aqueous solutions	ΔE_0
changes in surface tension in aqueous solutions	$\Delta \gamma$
changes in capillary actions of aqueous solutions	$\Delta h = 0, \ \Delta h \gg 0$
changes of the electric conductivity in aqueous solutions	$\Delta \sigma$
changes in the resistance of electric conductors	ΔR
changes in the hydrodynamic behaviour of water	Δ **Reynolds Number**
changes in half life times of radioactive isotopes	$\Delta \tau$
changes in chemical reaction rates	$\Delta \tau$
acceleration anomalies of NASA-spacecraft around celestial bodies	$\Delta g(r)$
emergence of non-electromagnetic electrosmog	**electrosmog**
generation of „free energy" from subtle energy	Δ **energy**

Consequences from the Theory of Subtle Matter	symbol
extended special and general theories of relativity	SR and GR
explanation of space-time (ST) and curvature of ST	spacetime
extended quantum mechanics	QM
explanation of the quantum paradoxes	QM
explanation of dark energy and dark matter	Δm
explanation of anomalies at celestial objects and black holes	astrophysics
extended thermodynamics and negentropic/ kinetic changes	Δ Gibbs-function extended
law of gravitation and uncertainty of G, fifth force	$\Delta G/G \gg \Delta e/e$
extension of Newton's law of gravity by subtle terms	gravity
explanation of anti-gravitative effects	gravity
extension of particle physics, transmutations (LENR)	particle physics
causal explanation of complementary medicine	medicine
causal explanation of astrological effects	universal subtle entanglement

5 Appendix

5.1 Quanta of Subtle Matter

The upper section of Table 1 lists the detected masses of subtle matter quanta as discovered to date. These quanta represent elementary "proto-particles" of a second subtle kind of matter having a field-like nature. This is in sharp contrast to the well known gross elementary point-like particles of modern physics. Also, in parentheses, their experimentally found errors are listed as 95 % confidence intervals, i.e. as "95 %-CI".

Table 1: Values of quanta of Subtle Matter

Experimentally found subtle quanta
$m_P = \pm 21.5\,\mu g\ (\pm 1.3\,\mu g\ 95\,\%\text{-CI})$
$m_S = \pm 1.87\,\mu g\ (\pm 0.19\,\mu g\ 95\,\%\text{-CI})$
$m_{SE} = \pm 0.36\,\mu g\ (\pm 0.02\,\mu g\ 95\,\%\text{-CI})$
Theoretical values from present day physics
$m_P = \pm(h \cdot c/(2 \cdot \pi \cdot G))^{0.5} = \pm 21.7\,\mu g$
$m_S = \pm(e^2/(4 \cdot \pi \cdot \varepsilon_0 \cdot G))^{0.5} = m_P \cdot \alpha^{0.5} = \pm 1.86\,\mu g$
$m_{SE} = \pm m_P \cdot (\alpha/(8 \cdot \pi))^{0.5} = m_S/(8 \cdot \pi)^{0.5} = \pm 0.37\,\mu g$

The lower section of the table gives the derivation of our detected values of subtle matter quanta using the natural constants of present day physics, i.e. the Planck mass

m_P = ±21.7 μg, the Stoney mass m_S = ±1.86 μg, and a previously unknown further basic mass, which we named, the Stoney/Einstein mass m_{SE} = ±0.37 μg.

This correlation between the experimentally found and theoretically described masses of the different subtle field-quanta, gives us, for the first time, a concrete "bridge" between subtle matter and the known physics of gross matter.

The results show that such subtle quanta can have a positive or negative physical sign, yielding therefore gravitational (with positive sign = weight increasing) or anti-gravitational, i.e. repulsive (with negative sign = weight reducing) effects in combination with gross matter. Negative sign field-quanta may also associate with each other by gravitational force, or possibly by other interactions.

As already mentioned, additional tests reveal that field-quanta can form clusters, just as atoms associate to form molecules, and that such clusters can rearrange themselves into new structures.

These findings support the proposal that subtle matter field-quanta (with a spatially extended field-like structure at the macroscopic scale) having a positive sign, are identical to the proposed „dark matter" or „cold dark matter". Similarly, field-quanta with a negative sign, may be identical to the proposed „dark energy". Effects of both dark energy and dark matter have been found in astrophysical observations, yet neither a bench scale proof of their existence, nor a theoretical framework for their description is available. At

CERN and other locations, both dark matter and dark energy are being searched for on the assumption that they are simply two more elementary particles within the Standard Model of modern physics.

5.2   Extension of the Law of Gravity

The observed, time-dependent, mass changes Δm of the described detectors with newly generated phase boundaries violate the first law of thermodynamics, i.e. conservation of mass and energy in isolated systems. The detected Δm-values finally approach a plateau over time.

Thus, all gross objects (i.e. minerals, metals or water) in the Universe are carrying subtle field-bodies (resulting from subtle matter with a positive sign, or subtle matter with a negative sign) with real mass, in a balanced state with the environment, including celestial bodies, being bound due to the form-specific interaction at phase boundaries and/or by gravity.

Thus, gravitational interactions occur not only between gross objects with mass m_g, but also between gross objects and their subtle field-bodies with mass m_s, and between the subtle field-bodies. This implies that Newton's law of gravity must be extended in the following way, see Table 2, that includes various spatially extended subtle field-masses that together may be associated with a single gross object:

Table 2: Extended Law of Gravity

$$F = G \cdot m_{1g} \cdot m_{2g}/r^2 \qquad \textit{classic gross-gross term} \quad (1)$$

$$\pm m_{1g} \cdot \Sigma_i G_i \cdot (\textstyle\int (m_{2si}(r) \cdot dr)/r_i{}^2 \qquad \textit{new gross-subtle term} \quad (2)$$

$$\pm \Sigma_{ij} G_{ij} \cdot [(\textstyle\int m_{1si}(r) \cdot dr) \cdot (\textstyle\int m_{2sj}(r) \cdot dr)]/(r_i - r_j)^2 \quad \textit{new subtle-} \quad (3) \\ \textit{subtle term}$$

$$\pm \Sigma_{ij} [\textstyle\int (m_{1si}(r) \cdot H \cdot m_{2sj}(r)]/r_{ij} \qquad \textit{new macroscopic QM-term} \quad (4)$$

The last term results from macroscopic or cosmic quantum mechanical superpositions of various field-bodies of two gross objects, where the $m_{si}(r)$-field acts like the orbitals in microscopic quantum mechanics, but now at the macroscopic or cosmic scale. This is because subtle field-bodies not only generate the effects of quantum mechanics at the microscopic level of atoms and molecules, but also at the macroscopic or at the cosmic astrophysical level (see below).

Whether or not Planck's quantum of action h can be used to tackle these new quantum mechanical effects at various scales is still an open question. By applying at least the first and second terms of the extended law of gravity, the mass deviations that lead to the proof of existence of subtle matter can be explained, thus avoiding "violations of the law of conservation of mass".

This holds also for explanations of the acceleration anomalies of NASA spacecraft NEAR Shoemaker in a flyby maneuver around Earth or of Pioneer 10 and 11 in the solar system. This implies, that the first law of thermodynamics applied to conservation of mass and energy in isolated systems must be extended by a subtle term, i.e. $\Sigma m_{gross} + \Sigma m_{subtle} = $ constant. However, it is not easy to establish an isolated system for subtle matter under laboratory bench scale conditions, because subtle matter easily penetrates all gross barriers.

By taking the Planck mass $m_P = +(\hbar \cdot c/(2 \cdot \pi \cdot G))^{0.5}$ and the Planck length $l_P = (\hbar \cdot G/(2 \cdot \pi \cdot c^3))^{0.5}$ into term No. (3) it reduces to the Planck force, i.e. $F_P = G \cdot m_P^2/l_P^2 = c^4/G$. Similarly, term No. (3) leads with m_S and $G \cdot m_S^2 = e^2/(4 \cdot \pi \cdot \varepsilon_0)$ from Table 1 to a deduction of Coulomb's law F_C, i.e. $F_C = G \cdot m_S^2/r^2 = e^2/(4 \cdot \pi \cdot \varepsilon_0 \cdot r^2)$, while the terms (1), (2) and (4) can be neglected.

This implies that a higher-dimensional extension of both Maxwell's equations and General Theory (GT, see below), should lead to a unified description of electromagnetic and gravitational forces, where for the non-relativistic limit the first three terms of the force F of Table 2 should result. This extension may be done by applying the coordinate sets $\{(x, y, z, i \cdot c \cdot t)/i^n\}$ with n either $n = 0$ and 1 or $n = 0$, 1 and 2, thus including effects of the 4-D_{U1}-gross and the 8-D_{U2}- or 12-D_{U2}-subtle level. For the simplest case, i.e. $n = 0$ and 1 of the space-set $\{4$-D_{U1}, 8-$D_{U2}\}$, the set of coordinates $\{x, y, z, i \cdot c \cdot t, x/i, y/i, z/i, c \cdot t\}$ and a metric with the diagonal terms $(1, -1, -1, -1, 1, -1, -1, -1)$ may be applicable.

Extension of GR:

Einstein's GR reduces in the non-relativistic case to Newton's law of gravity, i.e. the first term in the above equation. However, such a reduction does not describe the three additional terms, where field-bodies of subtle matter are involved. This implies, that GR should be extended to higher than 4 dimensions. Further research may reveal whether an 8- or 12-dimensional extension of GR can overcome this indulgence.

Inaccuracy of the Value of G:

Effects of the second term in the extended Law of gravity seem to play a significant role in the explanation of a major anomaly in modern physics. Usually, the relative error of Natural Constants is in the order of magnitude of $(\Delta h/h)/(\Delta e/e) = 2$ (see CODATA 2018). But the relative error of the gravitational constant G is significantly larger in comparison to, for example $\Delta e/e$, i.e. $(\Delta G/G)/(\Delta e/e) = 7607 \gg 2$.

This unusually large error results from a scattering of the determined data of G in various experiments in the past decades, see Nolting, F., et al., Europhysics News 31 (4), 25–27 (2000) (and cf. https://www.europhysicsnews.org/articles/epn/abs/2000/04/epn00406/epn00406.html).

Usually, the determination of G is done by applying a test device first described, by Cavendish (cf. https://en.wikipedia.org/wiki/Cavendish_experiment), where the oscillations of steel balls is studied, and where the masses, diameters and relative positions of the balls are very precisely determined, see, for example, https://asd.gsfc.nasa.gov/Stephen.Merkowitz/G/Big_G.html.

However, in such tests, the currently unknown subtle field-bodies which may be absorbed by the rotating steel balls are not taken into consideration. But, according to the second term in the extended law of gravity (in a first approach, maybe the other terms can be neglected, see above), such subtle fields associated with the steel balls, may vary from test to test, and may thus significantly disturb the measurement from one experiment to the next, producing significant variations in values for G.

Research in subtle matter has revealed that iron shows the strongest tendency to absorb subtle matter. Instead, to reduce the scattering effects in the determination of G, balls made of beryllium should be used because this element binds subtle matter to a very low degree, as research in subtle matter shows. Or, the steel balls could, prior to an experiment be treated with high intensity ultrasound shocks to shake off any absorbed subtle matter fields, because tests revealed that strong mechanical shocks lead to the desorption of subtle field-bodies that are bound to gross objects.

5.3   Extension of Thermodynamics

Thermodynamics describes the bulk behavior of systems of gross matter with respect to various possible (or impossible) energy transformations without giving details about the kinetics or velocities of such changes.

Zeroth Law of Thermodynamics states that equilibrium is given between systems A and C if A is in equilibrium with system B, and C also is in equilibrium with B. Temperature measurements under increased negentropic field-intensities show spontaneous temperature reductions while in greater entropic field-intensities elevated temperatures can be observed, thus violating zeroth law of thermodynamics.

First Law of Thermodynamics comprises the law of conservation of energy and mass under non-relativistic conditions in an isolated system. This holds true for systems of gross matter. Effects of subtle matter can violate this law, so that the law must be extended to $\sum m_{gross} + \sum m_{subtle}$ = constant.

Second Law of Thermodynamics states, for example, that in any spontaneously running process, total entropy (or in simple terms, "disorder") must increase in the Universe.

According to the second law of thermodynamics, spontaneously running processes can occur only, if for the "Gibbs-function ΔG" of the process a negative sign results, i.e. $\Delta G = [\Delta H - T \cdot \Delta S] < 0$. If we take subtle matter into consideration, this "classical" second law of thermodynamics (indicated by the index "gross", and neglecting effects of chemical potentials) must be extended by additional subtle matter terms (indicated by the index "subtle"), as shown here:

$$\Delta G = [\Delta H - T \cdot \Delta S]_{gross} + [\Delta H - T \cdot \Delta S]_{subtle}$$

Now, we must distinguish, in a spontaneously running process, between dominant effects of gross matter, where subtle effects can be neglected, and dominant effects of subtle matter, resulting from increased intensities of fields of subtle matter.

In thermodynamics of the past hundred years, the terms $[\Delta H - T \cdot \Delta S]_{subtle}$ could be neglected due to the usually very low intensity of subtle matter in any bench scale studies or in technical applications. Such subtle matter effects "vanished", so to say, in the experimental noise. But in reaching high intensities of subtle matter, due to specialized detectors where this field-like matter can be cumulatively absorbed to a significant degree, the situation in spontaneously running processes can change "dramatically".

Extension of the second Law of Thermodynamics to a "Fourth Law of Thermodynamics":

In principle, the above extended Gibbs-equation with subtle terms can be understood as a new, fourth law of thermodynamics. If the effects of subtle matter in ΔH_{subtle} and $T \cdot \Delta S_{subtle}$ are due to negentropic effects of fields of increased intensity, we can speak about a "principle of negentropy" or "syntropy", which can work in opposition to the classical second law of thermodynamics, because 73 % of the total mass of the Universe is built up of negentropic forms of subtle matter (possible equivalent to dark energy).

As described above, "negentropic, and thus, live-giving effects" should occur in the Universe in abundance, not only here on Earth, and not only in living systems as we know them. In 1944, Erwin Schrödinger postulated the existence of negentropic effects in living beings (cf. https://en.wikipedia.org/wiki/What_Is_ Life%3F), even though negentropic subtle matter was not known during this time.

In modern science "negentropic effects" are a kind of "taboo-topic" and are "substituted", so to speak, by gross, random, stochastic processes, which occur by chance, under the strict exclusion of negentropic effects. Such negentropic effects originate, as we now see, from sources of subtle universal "fields of negentropy", completely independent of gross matter. The Earth's global negentropic field-body, for example, could be quantitatively characterized in its structure and with its mass of about -10^{18} kg from the reported acceleration anomalies of NASA's NEAR Shoemaker spacecraft in its fly-by maneuver around Earth, thus confirming Sheldrake's phenomenological morphogenetic considerations.

The following pictures of an icesheet on a pond demonstrate the spontaneous form-generating morphic properties of subtle negentropy. The pond is located in the backyard of a company who is producing and selling "activated water" with a special method. The subtle "activation" of that water could be confirmed by our weighing experiments to exhibit a high intensity of negentropic subtle matter.

One day a surplus of this water was poured away into the small pond. In the next wintertime the surface of the pond froze over, and spontaneously highly ordered, flower-like structures with diameters of up to 100 centimeters took shape, without any external influence, yielding unique structures.

Fig. 55: Spontaneous form-generating effects of subtle negentropy in freezing icesheets (© Nova Vitalis GmbH)

Extension of Evolutionary Biology:

Another, and even more important, aspect of subtle negentropy, in accord with the extended Gibbs-function, affects biological evolution on Earth. In evolutionary biology it is assumed that by spontaneous "stochastic step-by-step mutations" and "selection of the fittest" the great sequence of diversified and branched species has been evolved in the long course of time from a primordial monad.

Nobel laureate **Ilya Prigogine's** irreversible thermodynamics provided a theoretical model of this evolutionary process, as schematically depicted in the following figure.

Open systems, with at least one internal non-linear process, like biological beings or a burning candle, exist in a thermodynamic stationary state ("state 1")

211

where their internal chemical processes generate in the course of time a total production of entropy S in a linear way, i.e. $\Delta S_A / \Delta t$ = constant, see line A. If external stochastic processes disturb such a system, so that $\Delta S_A / \Delta t$ would increase (see positions "a" or "c" in the graph), the internal non-linear processes have the ability to spontaneously eliminate this influence and to come back to original $\Delta S_A / \Delta t$-value of line A.

Fig. 56: Thermodynamic model according to Ilya Prigogine

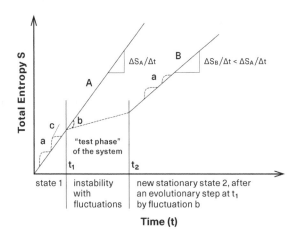

If we disturb, for example, a silently burning candle by soft movements of the hand, the candle starts to flicker and generates soot, i.e. $\Delta S_A / \Delta t$ is increased. But after a short while undisturbed, the candle comes back to its original smooth burning without the formation of soot, thus spontaneously eliminating the disturbance.

However, if an external or internal stochastic disturbance of the system leads to a reduction of $\Delta S_A / \Delta t$, the system becomes unstable, see position "b" at time t_1 in the graph, and after a test-phase with internal fluctuations, a new stationary state will be established at time t_2 where $\Delta S_B / \Delta t$ is reduced in comparison to the starting value of $\Delta S_A / \Delta t$. This implies an evolutionary step of the system. And in the long course of time, by such stochastic steps and following processes of selection, it is assumed in evolutionary biology, that even human beings have finally evolved from a unicellular single common ancestor in the past 3 billion years or so.

Research in subtle matter offers an additional process, because negentropic subtle disturbances from the Earth's global field-body (with a mass of about -10^{18} kg, see above) or from other field-bodies in the solar system (which exist, as quantitative research in subtle matter reveals), may have stimulated negentropic fluctuations in all kinds of living species in much higher frequencies and complexity, as purely stochastic fluctuations may have done. We should not forget, that the negentropic subtle global field-body is a self-aware, highly creative and intelligent field of consciousness. Instead of generating negentropic step-by-step fluctuations in an evolving living system every several thousand/million years or so, as described above, it is more likely that, according to changing environmental side-conditions of a species, in one stroke, and in an intelligent way, a complete self-consistent set of negentropic fluctuations could be triggered in a kind of "subtle mutagenic quantum-jump".

Such a process could explain the fact, about which even Charles Darwin pondered, that in the course of time, almost no "missing links" between related species could be found in paleontology. In other words, major jumps occur that can produce a new species.

Experiments with thermally killed plant seeds, which could be revived under increased negentropic field intensities (see Fig. 25), show that such an extended understanding of "complex evolutionary negentropic processes" exists, in accordance with the etherally extended second law of thermodynamics. The self-conscious, non-linear negentropic subtle matter may not only play a major role in chemical and biological evolution but also in the origion of life.

5.4   Understanding of Subtle Matter, Cosmology and Human Consciousness

The present day Standard Model of elementary particles which is based on Special Relativity is successful in describing point-like particles. However, it cannot be used to describe field-like forms of matter, where a single quantum of subtle matter may exhibit a spatial extension ranging over more than 10 cm around a central point. To achieve such a theoretical model, at least in principle, one can try to extend Special Relativity to higher dimensions.

To achieve this, the Minkowski concept to mathematically express the parameter of time t by $i \cdot c \cdot t$ can be generalized, by multiplying the usual set of coordinates, i.e. $\{x, y, z, i \cdot c \cdot t\}$, by a factor of $1/i^n$, where n is an integer number. Thus, introducing the generalized set of coordinates, i.e. $\{x, y, z, i \cdot c \cdot t\}/i^n$, to the well known procedure to deduce Special Relativity, one obtains three solutions with $n = 0, 1$ and 2, and where all other integers of n, i.e. $0 < n > 2$ turn out to be repetitions of the n-set $\{0, 1, 2\}$. This leads to a multidimensional cosmology as depicted schematically in Fig. 57, and yields for $n = 1$ a theoretical description of field-like subtle matter, while $n = 0$ and $n = 3$ describe subsystems of gross matter.

Fig. 57: The structure of existence and states of consciousness

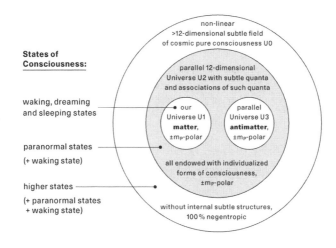

For $n = 0$ we get our visible 4-dimensional Universe, as denoted by U1, containing only normal gross matter. For $n = 1$ we have an invisible 12-dimensional parallel

Universe U2, that is completely filled with individualized forms of quanta and associations of such quanta of spatially extended field-like subtle matter, i.e. "$\pm m_P$", where m_P shall stand also for m_S and m_{SE} of Table 1 in Appendix 5.1, or for other so-far unknown subtle quanta, as well as associations of such quanta. For n = 2 one obtains a second 4-dimensional, yet invisible Universe U3, in parallel to U1, also as a subset of U2. It can be assumed that U1 and U3 emerged from U2 in a "twin-U1/U3-Big Bang". Due to symmetry reasons, U3 may only contain gross antimatter, exhibiting similar gross structures to those shown in U1.

It turns out that both, U1 and U3, emerge from two independent 4-dimensional subtle subsets, i.e. $U2_{sub1}$ and $U2_{sub3}$, of the 12-dimensional Universe U2. Both in U1 and in U3, effects of subtle matter may occur due to higher-dimensionality superimposed fields of subtle matter. Furthermore, it can be shown that U2 is a subset of a more basic >12-dimensional cosmological subtle level, i.e. U0, which encompasses the three Universes U1, U2 and U3.

It can be assumed, that U0 exhibits a 100 % negentropic quality, while the three Universes U1, U2 and U3 are pervaded by bipolar subtle negentropic and/or entropic $\pm m_P$-structures. Seen from an observer in U1, subtle matter and subtle field-bodies in $U2_{sub1}$ act in an 8-dimensional and trans-dimensional way from the level of $U2_{sub1}$ into our visible 4-dimensional Universe U1, where they can interact with gross matter through form-specific (i.e. topological) and gravitational interactions, so that they can be detected in weighing experiments as described above. Besides the two mentioned interactions, subtle matter also exhibits very weakly expressed electric and an also a weakly expressed magnetic interaction with gross matter. Because the electric charge of subtle quanta is very low in intensity, subtle matter is invisible to the naked human eye. But at universal scales all four interactions may interplay with gross bodies, even with celestial objects, so that one could speak about a "subtle Universe U1", an "electric Universe U1" or a "magnetic Universe U1".

Understanding altered States of Consciousness:
The cosmological concept of reality, as sketched and schematically depicted above can furthermore be used to define altered states of human consciousness.

The gross human nervous system and the body are only instruments of resonance to the higher-dimensionally superimposed subtle field-body in U2 which guides as a pilot-field human psyche as well as the microscopic metabolism in function, structure and morphology.

In the waking state the human eye has, in the visual process, only access to gross objects. However, if a human being becomes consciously aware (due to a refined nervous system) of the neuronal processes of the subtle Platonic beam which in the waking state is subconsciously emitted and recorded in the visual process, an extended paranormal state of consciousness becomes established. In this altered state of consciousness, besides gross objects also subtle matter fields and field-bodies can be recognized.

Furthermore, reports from a great number of people today, and throughout history reveal, that by an even more refined state of the neuronal system, a human being is able to consciously experience the level of U0, the field of Pure Consciousness and basis of all natural laws, allowing actions in accord with this basic field of nature.

5.5 Approach to the Introduction of a Universal Physical "Ether" Based on Subtle Matter

A consequence of the experimental verification of invisible space- and field-like subtle quanta and of the extension of the Special Theory of Relativity (SR) is the possibility to introduce in physics a universal subtle ether as the basis of universal spacetime. As is shown in short in the following, this allows the solution of various anomalies in present-day physics. On the one hand, Stephen Hawking states in the glossary of his book "The Universe in a Nutshell" (2001): "Ether: A hypothetical non-material medium once supposed to fill all space. The idea that such a medium is required for propagation of electromagnetic radiation is no longer tenable". On the other hand, Einstein, in his 1920 lecture at the University of Leiden (see Einstein, "Äther und Relativitäststheorie", Springer, speech of 27. Oct. 1920), concluded by stating:

"We may say that according to the general theory of relativity space is endowed with physical qualities; in this sense, therefore, there exists an ether. According to the general theory of relativity, space without ether is unthinkable; for in such space there not only would be no propagation of light, but also no possibility of existence for standards of space and time (measuring-rods and clocks), nor therefore any space-time intervals in the physical sense. But this ether may not be thought of as endowed with the quality characteristic of ponderable media, as consisting of parts which may be tracked through time. The idea of motion may not be applied to it."

Einstein continued proclaiming that the ether he was speaking about should be termed as "relativistic ether" or "new ether" to distinguish it from the "light-ether" thought of in the 19th century. It is remarkable that this statement of Einstein is ignored by Hawking and by the worldwide scientific community, and that, for example, no physical explanation for the curvature of spacetime (as basis of gravity, according to General Theory (GT)) is given in physics today because the assumed universal vacuum has no such property.

Based on the verification of field-like quanta of subtle matter, we hold onto Einstein's considerations and formulate, with the detected field-like quanta of subtle matter (see Table 1 in Appendix 5.1), a subtle universal, invisible yet real "relativistic ether" (see below), yielding an internal frame of the visible Universe instead of the present-day assumption of a "universal vacuum". Because it is known from astrophysical studies that universal spacetime exhibits at large scales an Euclidean structure, an orthogonal cubic $\pm m_P$-lattice with face-centered $\pm m_S$-quanta is chosen for the ether in which major coordinates intersect with angles of 90°, and where the neighboring quanta at Planck distances are held together by the Planck force $F_P = c^4/G$.

It can be shown that such a bosonic ether, where the $\pm m_P/\pm m_S$-quanta, with alternative signs and spins at the cubic and face-centered positions of the ether, is not only consistent with the well known relativistic and quantum-mechanical properties of gross matter, rather it will turn out that the relativistic ether is the essential basis to generate these properties of gross particles. And, as shown in the following, the developed understanding of an 8-dimensional (i.e. 8-D_{U2}) subtle parallel Universe U2, being superimposed onto the subset of our visible 4-D_{U1}-Universe U1, can be used to explain major anomalies in modern physics as outlined below.

1. Spacetime Is a Geometrically Structured Field of Subtle Matter: The introduced universal subtle ether allows a quantitative explanation of the reversible bending of spacetime as described in GT under the influence of gross masses, as searched for by Einstein, allows the explanation of the propagation of gravitational waves and replaces the currently assumed "universal vacuum". Thus all "physical fields" emerge from the universal ether as different physical aspects of the universal ethereal field of subtle matter, and the ether is regarded as being the carrier of all forms of gross matter and of all "virtual forces" between gross particles.

2. Explanation of the "Vacuum Catastrophe": The "vacuum energy" is regarded in present-day physics as an underlying background energy that exists in space throughout the entire Universe. The exact nature of the particles (or fields) that generate vacuum energy with a density as great as that required by inflation theory remains a mystery.

Using the upper limit of the cosmological constant, the vacuum energy of free space at the gross level has been estimated to be $\sim 10^{-9}$ J/m^3. However, both quantum electrodynamics and stochastical electrodynamics requires it to have a tremendously larger value of about 10^{113} J/m^3. This huge discrepancy between $\sim 10^{-9}$ J/m^3 and $\sim 10^{113}$ J/m^3 i.e. the ratio $10^{113}/10^{-9} = 10^{122} \gg 1$, is known as the "vacuum catastrophe". This anomaly has been described as "the worst theoretical prediction in the history of physics" (see Wikipedia for "Cosmological constant problem").

In the extended physics proposed here, the "vacuum" is replaced by the "relativistic ether", as mentioned. Based on the face-centered cubic elementary cell with Planck length, and on the absolute masses of the involved subtle $\pm m_P / \pm m_S$-quanta, a subtle density of the ether of 10^{113} J/m^3 results.

This result is in excellent agreement with the above value of about 10^{113} J/m^3, predicted, but unexplained in modern physics. Thus, while the above density of

10^{-9} J/m^3 is given at the gross 4-D_{U1}-level of U1, the value of 10^{113} J/m^3 exists at the subtle 8-D_{U2}-level of the parallel Universe U2 where inflation takes place, and which generates the basis of the visible Universe U1. Thus, it is a necessity that two different energy densities exist, one at the gross U1-level with $\sim10^{-9}$ J/m^3, and another one at the subtle U2-level with $\sim10^{113}$ J/m^3. This result gives credit, on the one hand, to the concept that a parallel Universe U2 exists superimposed onto, and pervading, the visible Universe U1, and supports, on the other hand, the existence of a subtle, relativistic 8-D_{U2}-ether as the basis of a universal 4-D_{U1}-spacetime that penetrates and underlies the visible Universe U1.

3. Prediction of the Rest Masses of Elementary Particles: Achieving "gross fermionic particles" as individual entities within the ether's universal bosonic structure requires local disturbances of a fermionic nature, such as localized rotational anomalies, due to spin switching within the ether to a local spin state ½ (yielding neutrinos with very low or no rest mass) or due to the formation of "$(+m_S/-m_S)$-vortices" from neighboring $\pm m_S$-quanta in the ether lattice which rotate around each other, again exhibiting a spin state of ½. In the thus developed 8-dimensional subtle / 4-dimensional gross-model of elementary particles, embedded in the universal ether, such $\pm m_S$-vortices are regarded as subtle core-structures of gross particles with rest mass m > 0. This model allows a quantitative prediction of the rest mass of gross elementary particles from their respective geometrical subtle core structures (see Fig. 58).

Fig. 58: Comparison of the experimentally detected rest masses of gross elementary "4-D_{U1}-particles" and predicted values, deduced from their subtle 8-D_{U2}-core-structures, relative to the electron's rest mass m_e. In the case of a perfect fit all values should lie on the 45° intersection. In the areas where no subtle 8-D_{U2}-core structures can be geometrically constructed, no gross 4-D_{U1}-particles exist (see the shaded squares). Together with the excellent fit of the data, this gives credit to the developed 8-dimensional subtle/4-dimensional gross-model of elementary particles, where the gross particles express only the gross "iceberg-tips" (i.e. the gross 4-D_{U1}-components) of the total entity of an 8-dimensional androgynous 8-D_{U2}-subtle/4-D_{U1}-gross particle.

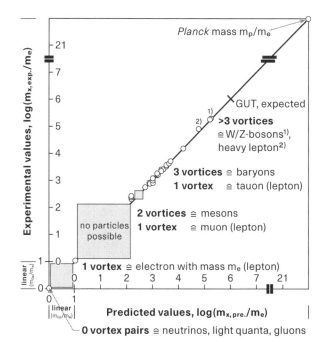

4. Common Deduction of ST and QM, Explanation of QM as well as of the Quantum Paradoxes: The presented androgynous (8-dimensional subtle/4-dimensional gross)-model of elementary particles embedded in the universal ether allows a common quantitative deduction of the quantum mechanical properties of gross elementary particles as well as their relativistic behavior, thus revealing that the introduced ether is a "relativistic ether", as postulated by Einstein.

Furthermore, it follows from the deduced particle model that quantum mechanical chemical orbitals and eigenstates are real standing waves of subtle matter, and that all of quantum mechanics, in general, results from the subtle 8-dimensional field-components of the gross 4-dimensional particle components.

In addition, this particle model allows a physical explanation of the previously unexplained, yet predicted and measured, quantum paradoxes such as, for example, the explanation of the wave/particle duality (i.e. the $8\text{-}D_{U2}$-field-/$4\text{-}D_{U1}$-particle-components), of the results of double slit experiments or of the entanglement in EPR-entanglements, which-way experiments, etc. This concept is, in addition, consistent with David Bohm's formulation of the "quantum mechanics of hidden (i.e. subtle) variables" based on the idea of an "implicate" (i.e. subtle) order in U2, yielding an excited "explicate" (i.e. gross) order in U1.

5. Explanation of Quarks and the Broken Charges of Quarks: This 8-dimensional subtle/4-dimensional gross-model of elementary particles allows a quantitative explanation of the broken electric charges $+\frac{2}{3}$, and $-\frac{1}{3}$ of up/charm/top- and down/strange/bottom-quarks.

Titled "Quarks are still elusive", CERN published in the CERN Courier (52, (3), April 2012, p. 16) that with latest accelerator technology, according to the standard model of elementary particles, down to a scattering cross section of 10^{-39} cm^2, no particles with electric $(\frac{1}{3})$- or $(\frac{2}{3})$-charges could be detected, leading to the statement: "It can be concluded that the likelihood to observe quarks with the existing accelerators is very low". Detailed research in the subtle background structures of gross elementary particles reveals that the present-day postulated quarks are identical to $\pm m_S$-vortices of pairs of subtle $\pm m_S$-quanta that spin around each other. Also the electron itself results from a single field-quantum $\pm m_S$-vortex, thus expressing a "quark". The broken electric charges of present-day assumed quarks result quantitatively from the geometrical structures of the subtle matter background components of leptons or baryons and a primordial electric charge of $e/2$. This primordial electric charge is, however, bound to the subtle m_S-vortex-quanta of gross particles and cannot be detected in accelerators like CERN. Similarly, the spins $(\frac{1}{2}) \cdot h/(2 \cdot \pi)$ of the gross elementary particles, like leptons or baryons, result from primordial spins $(\frac{1}{4}) \cdot h/(2 \cdot \pi)$ that are also associated to the m_S-vortex-quanta.

6. Prediction of the Values of Natural Constants: The 8-dimensional subtle/4-dimensional gross-model of elementary particles allows a quantitative prediction of the values of the following natural constants:

Table 3: Predicted Values of Natural Constants

A: Sommerfeld's fine structure constant α

$\alpha = 2 \cdot \pi \cdot e^2 / (4 \cdot \pi \cdot \varepsilon_0 \cdot h \cdot c) = (32 / (8 \cdot \pi \cdot 0.024322 \cdot 15 \cdot 16^4))^{0.5}$
$\quad = 1/137.035 \ldots$

B: Electric charge

$e = \pm [h \cdot c \cdot \alpha \cdot (4 \cdot \pi \cdot \varepsilon_0) / (2 \cdot \pi)]^{0.5} = 1.60219 \cdot 10^{-19} \, C$

C: Bohr magneton

$\mu_B = (1/2) \cdot e \cdot h / (2 \cdot \pi \cdot m_e) = 9.2742 \cdot 10^{-24} \, J \cdot m^2 / (V \cdot s)$

---

7. Explanation of "Electrosmog": The 8-dimensional subtle/4-dimensional gross-model of elementary particles allows a quantitative explanation of electrosmog and its physical effects. Due to this model, quantized gross eigenstates in the visible Universe U1 are directly correlated with superimposed subtle eigenstates with identical energies in 8-D_{U2}-fields as subsystems of the 12-D_{U2}-spacetime.

This implies, for example, that in the deexitation of an electronic 4-D_{U1}-eigenstate, not only does an energetic change of the gross point-like component take place, accompanied by the emission of an electromagnetic $h \cdot v$-quantum, but also a similar energetic change of the subtle matter 8-D_{U2}-component takes place which generates the excited orbital where the electron's gross component was embedded. This implies the emission of a subtle, non-electromagnetic form of radiation, $h_s \cdot v_s$, in addition to the electromagnetic one.

Because of physical side conditions, this subtle emission has a positive sign, and implies health-destroying (entropic) properties if this form of radiation is, for example, absorbed by a living system. This kind of so-far scientifically unknown form of radiation, i.e. $+h_s \cdot v_s$, is the cause of so-called "electrosmog" in connection with all de-excitation processes in electric systems as well as at the nuclear level. Especially dramatic effects of electrosmog exist, for example, in the neighborhood of nuclear power plants (NPP) or of final disposal sites of nuclear wastes. In two independent studies conducted by the German "Federal Office for Radiation Protection" in 2007 and 2008, it was found that within an area of about 5 km around NPPs the likelihood of children falling sick with leukemia is increased by 100 %.

Reasons for this effect are today scientifically unknown, because all radioactive forms of α-, β-, or γ-radiation are completely blocked inside modern NPPs, and elevated values cannot be detected in their neighborhood. However, in the process of de-excitation of the radioactive fuel in NPPs, not only is useful heat generated by the decomposition of fissionable material, but also non-electromagnetic subtle matter radiation with a positive sign, i.e. "electrosmog", is released in high intensity.

This radiation is passing through the gross shielding materials for the electromagnetic forms of radiation without resistance. It is absorbed where new phase boundaries are generated at high rates. That is because, at newly generated phase boundaries, subtle matter is absorbed especially well. This is the case in the cellular growth process of young children, and therefore leads to their increased morbidity, while in adults with lower cell production obviously the immune system can handle the situation.

8. Experimental Tests reveal that increased intensities of fields of subtle matter allow:

A: the generation of free energy from subtle matter at a technical scale,

B: the study of transmutations of chemical elements in LENR-processes either to isotopes or to other elements at room temperature and at normal pressure, and

C: an approach to study anti-gravitational effects at the laboratory or technical scale.

5.6 Subtle Matter – a Vision of Possible Applications

Tests performed with modern, automatic-weighing technologies of high precision reveal the existence of a previously unknown form of subtle matter with macroscopic mass and energy. The new form of matter is invisible and field-like, yet it can be absorbed by special detectors and likely can be used, for example, for the generation of "free energy".

The new form of subtle matter also opens a door for a deeper understanding of life, consciousness, collective consciousness, and evolution. Furthermore, the detection of various quanta of subtle matter leads to the formulation of a **subtle-matter extended new physics**. The extended new physics explains many present-day physical anomalies and covers, among others, the following topics:

▷ **Extended space-time-physics, existence of a universal subtle Ether:** Explanation of a variety of gravitational anomalies, such as anomalies during solar eclipses; extended law of gravitation: explanation of the large error of Newton's gravitational constant G; explanation of space-time curvature and of the mechanism of gravitation; explanation of the postulated "dark energy" and "dark matter" based on bench scale tests revealing what appear to be subtle matter-fields with negative and positive signs; deduction of the 1st and 2nd axioms of Newton's mechanics;

▷ **Extended physics of elementary particles:** Explanation of the formation of matter; prediction of the rest masses of elementary particles and of various natural constants; explanation of quantum mechanics and of quantum paradoxes; mutual deduction of microscopic quantum mechanics and special relativity, from an extended model of elementary particles; deduction of Coulomb's law;

▷ **Extended physics of the solar system:** Solar, lunar and global effects of subtle matter, i.e.

explanation of so-far not understood acceleration anomalies of solar and global NASA spacecraft;

▷ **Extended astrophysics:** Realization of a cosmic subtle matter quantization in addition to a macroscopic quantization of field-bodies and besides the well-known microscopic quantization, all resulting from associated fields of subtle matter; explanation of the structures of planetary nebulae and their dynamic effects, such as bipolar jet-streams of young and old stars, as well as of black holes or stellar galactic orbitals;

▷ **Extended cosmology:** Proof of the existence of three Universes in parallel;

▷ **Extended chemistry:** Subtle matter explanations of chemical orbitals and of electrosmog;

▷ **Extended biology:** Subtle matter explanation of the phenomena of life and consciousness; establishment of a macroscopic quantum mechanics in biology and in association with complementary medicine; realization of the superluminal astrological entanglement of all forms of life in a living Universe, thus supporting the teleological connection of the field-bodies of all forms of life with the field-bodies of astrophysical objects;

▷ **Extended medicine:** Proof of existence of the human invisible, yet real, subtle matter field-body and causal explanation of complementary medicine, as well as of natural healing methods including homeopathy; explanation of "negentropically activated water"; subtle matter extended sensory perception;

▷ **Extended understanding of evolution:** Extension of "Darwin's theory of evolution";

▷ **Extended technologies and economics:** Large scale recovery of free energy from subtle matter field-energy without damaging the environment and the world's climate; transmutations at technological levels as well as research in negentropically dominated anti-gravity technologies.

Made in the USA
Columbia, SC
28 September 2020